T0301720

VALUATION IN A WORLD OF
CVA, DVA, AND FVA

A Tutorial on Debt Securities and Interest Rate Derivatives

VALUATION IN A WORLD OF CVA, DVA, AND FVA

A Tutorial on Debt Securities and Interest Rate Derivatives

Donald J Smith
Questrom School of Business, Boston University, USA

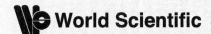

World Scientific

EW JERSEY · LONDON · SINGAPORE · BEIJING · SHANGHAI · HONG KONG · TAIPEI · CHENNAI · TOKYO

Published by

World Scientific Publishing Co. Pte. Ltd.

5 Toh Tuck Link, Singapore 596224

USA office: 27 Warren Street, Suite 401-402, Hackensack, NJ 07601

UK office: 57 Shelton Street, Covent Garden, London WC2H 9HE

British Library Cataloguing-in-Publication Data
A catalogue record for this book is available from the British Library.

VALUATION IN A WORLD OF CVA, DVA, AND FVA
A Tutorial on Debt Securities and Interest Rate Derivatives

ISBN 978-981-3222-74-8
ISBN 978-981-3224-16-2 (pbk)

Desk Editor: Shreya Gopi

Typeset by Stallion Press
Email: enquiries@stallionpress.com

Printed in Singapore

Contents

Introduction

The financial crisis of 2007–09 fundamentally changed the valuation of financial derivatives. Counterparty credit risk became central. Before September 2008, the thought of a major investment bank going into bankruptcy was unthinkable. Post-Lehman, that risk is a critical element in the valuation process. Bank funding costs rose dramatically during the crisis. A proxy for bank funding and credit risk is the LIBOR-OIS spread (LIBOR is the London Interbank Offered Rate and OIS is the Overnight Indexed Swap rate). That spread was 8–10 basis points before the crisis, peaked at 358 basis points at the time of the Lehman default, and has since stabilized but still remains above the pre-crisis level.

In addition to recognizing the impact of credit risk and funding costs to banks, regulatory authorities since the crisis have imposed new rules on capital reserves and margin accounts. This has led to a series of valuation adjustments to derivatives and debt securities, collectively known as the "XVA". These include CVA (credit valuation adjustment), DVA (debit, or debt, valuation adjustment), FVA (funding valuation adjustment), KVA (capital valuation adjustment), LVA (liquidity valuation adjustment), TVA (taxation valuation adjustment), and MVA (margin valuation adjustment). A problem, however, is that the models used in practice to calculate the XVA are very mathematical, and sometimes dauntingly so.

This book, which is essentially a tutorial, attempts to lay a foundation for "mathematically challenged" persons to understand the XVA, in particular, CVA, DVA, and FVA. As a basic description, "mathematically challenged" is when one (like the author) is comfortable with equations containing summation signs but struggles with expressions having integrals, especially with Greek letters and variables that have subscripts and superscripts.

Derivatives valuation is inherently difficult, starting with the famous Black-Scholes-Merton option-pricing model. I have a personal connection to this. I took a finance course in the Ph.D. program at the University of California at Berkeley with Mark Rubenstein in 1978. He, along with John Cox and Steve Ross, introduced the binomial option pricing model in a seminal paper, "Option Pricing: A Simplified Approach," in the *Journal of Financial Economics* in 1979. In that course, I believe we were among of the first students to ever see how options can be priced using binomial trees. I have often quipped that they developed the binomial model to get their "mathematically challenged" students (like me) to appreciate the assumptions that underlie Black-Scholes-Merton.

Nowadays the back-office quants employ "XVA engines" to value debt securities and derivatives, typically using Monte Carlo simulations that track many thousands of projected outcomes. This book uses a simple binomial tree model to replicate an XVA engine. The idea is that the values for the bond or interest rate derivative in the tree can be calculated using a spreadsheet program. This mimics its grown-up, real-world cousins used in practice. The book introduces the key parameters that drive CVA, DVA, and FVA (the expected exposure to default loss, the probability of default, and the recovery rate) and demonstrates the impact of changes in credit risk on values of various types of debt securities and interest rate derivatives in a simplified format using diagrams and tables, albeit with some mathematics. To be sure, the calculation of the XVA is in reality much more complex and much harder than is presented here.

Fortunately, there are several recently published books that go into the topic in depth and in all the mathematical detail needed to calculate the XVA in practice. These include:

- Jon Gregory, *The xVA Challenge: Counterparty Credit Risk, Funding, Collateral, and Capital*, 3rd Edition, (Wiley, 2015)
- Andrew Green, *XVA: Credit, Funding and Capital Valuation Adjustments*, (Wiley, 2016)
- Ignacio Ruiz, *XVA Desks — A New Era for Risk Management*, (Palgrave Macmillan, 2015)
- Dongsheng Lu, *The XVA of Financial Derivatives: CVA, DVA & FVA Explained*, (Palgrave Macmillan, 2016)

Perhaps the best statement about the mathematics behind XVA is the academic credentials of these authors. Jon Gregory has a Ph.D. in theoretical chemistry from the University of Cambridge. Andrew Green has a Ph.D. in theoretical physics, also from the University of Cambridge. Ignacio Ruiz got a Ph.D. in nano-physics from, again, the University of Cambridge. Dongsheng Lu received his Ph.D. in theoretical chemistry from Ohio State University. These authors are not mathematically challenged!

There are two primary sources for this book. The first is Frank Fabozzi's use of a binomial forward rate tree model to explain the valuation of embedded options. This appeared in 1996 in the third edition of his textbook, *Bond Markets, Analysis, and Strategies*, which now is in its ninth edition for 2015. Binomial tree models have been used in the CFA®️ (Chartered Financial Analyst) curriculum since 2000 and, therefore, are familiar to many finance professionals.

There is a key difference between the binomial forward rate tree model in the Fabozzi books and that presented herein. Fabozzi's primary objective is to demonstrate the impact of an embedded call or put option on the value of the underlying bond. Therefore, the interest rate that is modeled is the issuer's own bond yield because that rate drives the decision to exercise the option. The underlying bonds that are used to build the forward rate tree pertain to that issuer. The model also is used to value floating-rate notes and derivatives such as an interest rate cap but for these it is more of an abstraction because, in practice, they are not linked to the issuer's own cost of borrowed funds. Instead, they are tied to a benchmark such as LIBOR or a Treasury yield.

The forward rate modeled here is explicitly the benchmark rate and is based on the prices and coupon payments for a sequence of hypothetical government bonds. The benchmark rate by assumption represents the risk-free rate of interest, whereby "risk-free" refers to default but not inflation. The advantage to this assumption is that the binomial model produces the value of the bond or derivative assuming no default. Then an adjustment for credit risk, which is modeled separately, is subtracted to produce the *fair value*, that is, the value inclusive of credit risk. This approach is particularly relevant for floating-rate notes and interest rate derivatives that have cash flows linked to a benchmark rate. A disadvantage is that the model captures only part of the value of an embedded call or put option because the credit spread over the benchmark rate is assumed to be constant over the time to maturity. Holders of such embedded options in practice can benefit if the credit spread over the benchmark rate changes (narrowing on callable bonds and widening on putables).

The second source is John Hull's use of a table to demonstrate how the implied probability of default can be inferred from the price spread between a risky and a risk-free bond, given an assumption for the recovery rate. This is presented in the sixth edition of his textbook, *Options, Futures, and other Derivatives* (2006), currently in its ninth edition for 2014. Here a similar tabular method is used to calculate the CVA, DVA, and FVA given assumptions about the probability of default and the recovery rate. An innovation in this tutorial is that the binomial forward rate tree is used to get the expected exposure given default. That allows for analysis of the impact of interest rate volatility on the valuations.

This book makes no attempt to explain or teach credit risk analysis per se.[1] The key summary data on credit risk — the probability of default and the recovery rate if default occurs — are taken as given, as if those numbers are produced by credit analysts and given to the valuation team as inputs for further work. This work might be to set bid and ask prices for a trading group or to produce financial reports and statements for investors or risk managers. The probability of default could come from a credit rating agency, from the historical record on comparable securities, from a structural credit risk model, or from prices on credit default swaps.[2] The recovery rate reflects the status of the bond or derivative in the priority of claim (i.e., junior versus senior), the amount and quality of unencumbered assets available to creditors, and any collateralization agreement. Clearly, there are many legal and regulatory matters that have to be taken into account in determining the assumed default probability and recovery rates. The objective here is to obtain fair values for the debt securities and derivatives given the extent of credit risk as embodied in those key parameters.

A limitation of the model is that the credit risk parameters are assumed for simplicity to be independent of the level of benchmark interest rates for each future date. In reality, market rates and the business cycle are positively correlated by means of monetary policy. When the economy is strong — and presumably the probability of default by corporate debt issuers is low — interest rates tend to be higher because the central bank is tightening the supply of money and credit. When the economy is weak and default probabilities are high, expansionary monetary policy lowers benchmark rates.

Chapter I introduces the reader to valuation using a binomial forward rate tree. Two methods are shown — backward induction and pathwise valuation. The particular binomial forward rate tree used in Chapter I is derived in the Appendix, which demonstrates how the rates within the tree are calibrated by trial-and-error search. The model employs several simplifying assumptions to facilitate presentation, in particular, annual payment bonds and no accrued interest. The short-term interest rate refers to a 1-year benchmark bond yield. It should be clear, however, that computer technology allows the time frame to be collapsed to whatever degree of precision is needed, as well as to include complexity caused by various day-count conventions, accrued interest, and other complicating realities. This exposition employs an "artisanal approach" to model building in order to demonstrate what is going on inside the programming used in practice to value actual debt securities and derivatives.

Chapter II focuses on traditional fixed-rate corporate (or sovereign) bonds not having any embedded options. The binomial forward rate tree model is used to calculate the bond value assuming no default, denoted VND. Then a credit risk model is used to get the CVA and DVA given assumptions about default probability and recovery rates. The fair value for the corporate bond is the value assuming no default minus the adjustment for credit risk of the bond issuer, i.e., the VND minus the CVA or DVA. Then, given the fair value, the yield to maturity and the spread over the comparable-maturity benchmark bond are calculated. The objective is to assess the credit risk component to the yield and the spread. The forward rate tree model is then used to illustrate the calculation of the risk statistics (i.e., effective duration and convexity) for a traditional fixed-rate corporate bond. In addition, some fair value financial accounting issues are discussed.

Chapter III applies the same valuation methodology to floating-rate notes, first for a straight floater that pays a money market reference rate (here the 1-year benchmark rate) plus a fixed margin, and then for a capped floater that sets a maximum rate paid to the investor. The value of the embedded interest rate cap is inferred from the difference in the fair values of the straight and capped floaters. This is then compared to a standalone interest rate cap. The key point is that the credit risks of the issuer of capped floater and the standalone option contract can drive the decision to issue (or buy) the structured note having the embedded option or to issue (or buy) the straight floater and then separately acquire protection from higher reference rates.

Chapter IV demonstrates how the binomial tree model can be used to value a callable corporate bond under the limiting assumption of a constant credit spread over time. First, the bond is valued assuming that it is not callable — the VND and CVA/DVA determine the fair value. Then the constant spread over the 1-year benchmark rates is calculated. That produces the future values for the bond that signal if and when the call option is to be exercised by the issuer. Based on the specific call structure, i.e., the call prices and dates, the fair value and the option-adjusted spread (OAS) of the callable bond are obtained. The effective duration and convexity statistics for the callable bond are also calculated.

Chapter V covers interest rate swaps that have *bilateral* credit risk in contrast to the *unilateral* credit risk for traditional corporate fixed-rate, floating-rate, and callable bonds. A typical interest rate swap has a value of zero at inception but later can have positive or negative value as time passes and swap market rates and credit risks change. Therefore, the credit risk of both counterparties enters the valuation equation. An important result in the section is that the adjustments for credit risk (the CVA and DVA) can differ even if the counterparties have the same assumed probability of default and recovery rate. The difference arises from the expected exposure to default loss, which depends on the level and shape to the benchmark bond yield curve as embodied in the binomial tree. Numerical examples are used to illustrate the extent to which an interest rate swap can be valued as a long/short combination of fixed-rate and floating-rate bonds and as a combination of interest rate cap and floor agreements.

Chapter VI introduces FVA, the funding valuation adjustment that is used with derivatives portfolios but not with debt securities. FVA arises when non-collateralized swaps entered with corporate counterparties are hedged with collateralized swaps with other dealers. The interest rate paid or received on the cash collateral is lower than the bank's cost of borrowed funds in the money market. This gives rise to funding benefits when collateral is received and funding costs when it is posted to the counterparty or the central clearinghouse. This is the standard explanation for FVA although the XVA authors cited above go into other circumstances when funding costs and benefits arise in banking. Two possible methods to calculate FVA are demonstrated in the chapter.

Chapter VII demonstrates how the binomial forward rate tree model can be used to value and assess the price risk on two structured notes, an inverse floater and a bear floater. These are variations of a traditional floating-rate note. Instead of paying a reference rate *plus* some fixed rate, an inverse floater pays a fixed rate *minus* the reference rate. A bear floater pays a *multiple* to the reference rate *minus* a fixed rate. These structured notes have risk statistics quite unlike more traditional debt securities. To conclude, Chapter VIII contains summary statements about the key observations and results found in this manuscript.

This book started as a tutorial for the Fixed Income Markets courses that I teach for undergraduate and MBA students at the Questrom School of Business at Boston University. After the financial crisis, I knew that I needed to cover credit risk in much greater detail. I have found that these binomial trees and the credit risk tables are a perfect vehicle for this. Plus, many students love to do exercises using Excel. I self-published the tutorial in 2015 using CreateSpace, an Amazon subsidiary. Now I am pleased to revise and extend it into this book for World Scientific.

I would like to acknowledge the many students and colleagues who have helped me with this project. SunJoon Park and Zhenan (Micky) Li double-checked the calculations in the original tutorial. James Adams, Shayla Griffin, Eric Drumm, and Eddie Riedl gave me useful comments. Omar Yassin, Gunwoo Nan, and Zilong Zheng built creative Excel spreadsheet models with macros to produce the binomial trees. For this book, my research assistant, Kristen Abels, did an incredible job at proof-reading the manuscript and replicating all the numbers on her own spreadsheets. I am responsible for the remaining misstatements and errors. I would also like to thank Shreya Gopi, my editor at World Scientific, for her work on this manuscript.

Endnotes

1. Duffie and Singleton (2003) provide a rigorous presentation of credit risk for academicians and practitioners.
2. See, for example, the default probabilities and analysis of credit risk produced by Kamakura Corporation, www.kamakuraco.com.

About the Author

Donald J. Smith is from Long Island, New York, but graduated from high school in Honolulu, Hawaii. He attended San Jose State University, earning a BA in Economics and having spent a study abroad year in Uppsala, Sweden. He served as a Peace Corps volunteer in Peru and then went on to get an MBA and Ph.D. in applied economics from the University of California at Berkeley. His doctoral dissertation was on a theory of credit union decision-making. Don has been at Boston University for over 35 years, teaching fixed income markets and financial risk management. He is the author of *Bond Math: The Theory behind the Formulas*, 2nd Edition (Wiley Finance, 2014) and currently is a curriculum consultant to the CFA Institute.

This book is dedicated to Greyhounds and their Rescuers — "Every ex-racer that makes it from the track to a sofa is a winner."

Chapter I

An Introduction to Bond Valuation Using a Binomial Tree

I.1: Valuation of a Default-Risk-Free Bond Using a Binomial Tree with Backward Induction

Suppose that our challenge is to value a 5-year, 3.25%, annual payment, default-risk-free bond. I will illustrate the valuation process using the binomial forward rate tree shown in Exhibit I-1. Below each rate is the probability of arriving at that node. On Date 0 the 1-year rate is known, so its probability is 1.00. This model assumes that the odds of the rate going up and down at each node are 50–50. Therefore, the two rates for Date 1 each have a probability of 0.50. The Date-2 rates are 5.1111%, 3.4261%, and 2.2966% with probabilities of 0.25, 0.50, and 0.25, respectively. This is a recombinant tree so the middle rate can arise from the either of the Date-1 nodes. The Date-3 rates are 6.5184%, 4.3694%, 2.9289%, and 1.9633% with probabilities of 0.125, 0.375, 0.375, and 0.125, respectively. For Date 4, the rates are 8.0842%, 5.4190%, 3.6324%, 2.4349%, and 1.6322% with corresponding probabilities of 0.0625, 0.25, 0.375, 0.25, and 0.0625.

The calibration and underlying assumptions for the tree are detailed in the Appendix. In brief, the idea is to assume a probability distribution for 1-year forward interest rates (here, a lognormal distribution), a constant level of interest rate volatility (in this tree, 20%), and an underlying set of benchmark bonds. This is an arbitrage-free model in the sense that the values produced equal the known prices for the benchmark bonds. The benchmark bonds

Exhibit I-1: Binomial Forward Rate Tree for 20% Volatility

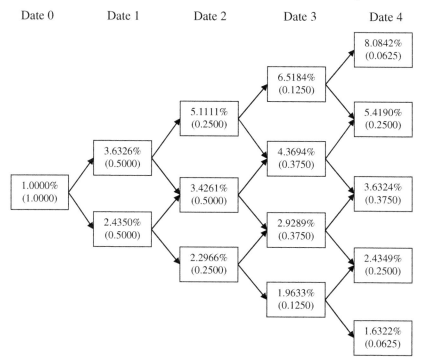

are presented in Exhibit I-2. Each of the five bonds is priced at par value so that the coupon rates and the yields to maturity are the same. This sequence of yields on par value bonds is known as the *benchmark par curve*.

From the par curve, we can bootstrap the sequence of *discount factors*, *spot rates*, and *forward rates*. These are shown in Exhibit I-3; the calculations are in the Appendix. A discount factor is the present

Exhibit I-2: Underlying Benchmark Coupon Rates, Prices, and Yields

Date	Coupon Rate	Price	Yield to Maturity
1	1.00%	100	1.00%
2	2.00%	100	2.00%
3	2.50%	100	2.50%
4	2.80%	100	2.80%
5	3.00%	100	3.00%

Exhibit I-3: Discount Factors, Spot Rates, and Forward Rates

Time Frame	Discount Factor	Spot Rate
0×1	0.990099	1.0000%
0×2	0.960978	2.0101%
0×3	0.928023	2.5212%
0×4	0.894344	2.8310%
0×5	0.860968	3.0392%

Time Frame	Forward Rate
0×1	1.0000%
1×2	3.0303%
2×3	3.5512%
3×4	3.7658%
4×5	3.8766%

value of one unit of money received at some time in the future. Spot (or zero-coupon) rates contain the same information as the corresponding discount rates. For instance, the 3-year discount factor and spot rate are 0.928023 and 2.5212%; they are denoted by the "0 × 3" (usually stated verbally as "0 by 3"). The first number is the beginning of the time frame and the second is the end. One can always derive a discount factor from a spot rate and vice versa.

$$\frac{1}{(1.025212)^3} = 0.928023$$

$$\left(\frac{1}{0.928023}\right)^{1/3} - 1 = 0.025212$$

The "4 × 5" forward rate of 3.8766% is the 1-period rate between Times 4 and 5. It begins at Time 4 and ends at Time 5. The forward rates, which comprise the *forward curve*, are calculated from either the discount factors or spot rates.

$$\frac{0.894344}{0.860968} - 1 = 0.038766$$

$$\frac{(1.030392)^5}{(1.028310)^4} - 1 = 0.038766$$

All calculations in this book are done on an Excel spreadsheet and the rounded values are reported in the text. Generally, discount factors are easier to use than spot rates when working with a spreadsheet. As shown in the Appendix, the binomial tree is calibrated to spread out around the forward curve in a manner that is consistent with no arbitrage and assumptions regarding the probability distribution and the assumed level of interest rate volatility.

While the intent of this section is to demonstrate how the bond is valued using a binomial tree, it is important to first note that the value can be calculated more directly using the discount factors, spot rates, or the forward rates. Given the underlying assumption of no arbitrage in the bootstrapping process, the value of the 5-year, 3.25%, annual payment bond is simply the present value of its scheduled cash flows. Using the discount factors, it is 101.1586 (per 100 of par value):

$$(3.25 * 0.990099) + (3.25 * 0.960978) + (3.25 * 0.928023)$$
$$+ (3.25 * 0.894344) + (103.25 * 0.860968) = 101.1586$$

The spot rates give the same result (when done on a spreadsheet and linking in the rates):

$$\frac{3.25}{(1.010000)^1} + \frac{3.25}{(1.020101)^2} + \frac{3.25}{(1.025212)^3} + \frac{3.25}{(1.028310)^4}$$
$$+ \frac{103.25}{(1.030392)^5} = 101.1586$$

The forward rates also give the same value (when done on a spreadsheet):

$$\frac{3.25}{(1.010000)} + \frac{3.25}{(1.010000 * 1.030303)}$$
$$+ \frac{3.25}{(1.010000 * 1.030303 * 1.035512)}$$
$$+ \frac{3.25}{(1.010000 * 1.030303 * 1.035512 * 1.037658)}$$

$$+ \frac{103.25}{(1.010000 * 1.030303 * 1.035512 * 1.037658 * 1.038766)}$$
$$= 101.1586$$

These calculations confirm that the discount factors, spot rates, and forward rates contain the same information about the benchmark par curve.

Exhibit I-4 demonstrates the result that the Date-0 value of the 5-year, 3.25%, annual payment government bond is also 101.1586 per 100 of par value when calculated on a binomial tree. To get that value, we start on Date 5 and work back to Date 0 through a process known as *backward induction*. Regardless of which of the five possible forward rates prevails on Date 4, the final coupon payment and principal redemption is 103.25. Those amounts are placed to the right of five Date-4 nodes in the tree. Next, the five possible values for the bond on Date 4 are calculated by discounting 103.25 by the

Exhibit I-4: Valuation of a 5-Year, 3.25%, Annual Payment Bond Using Backward Induction

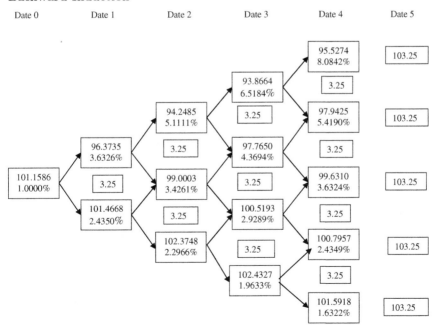

forward rates:

$$\frac{103.25}{1.080842} = 95.5274$$

$$\frac{103.25}{1.054190} = 97.9425$$

$$\frac{103.25}{1.036324} = 99.6310$$

$$\frac{103.25}{1.024349} = 100.7957$$

$$\frac{103.25}{1.016322} = 101.5918$$

Notice the well-known property that bond prices are inversely related to interest rates.

Now we can work backward to get the four possible bond values for Date 3. The coupon payment of 3.25 (per 100 of par value) due on Date 4 is placed to the right of the Date-3 forward rates. This format is used in all the binomial trees in this book: (1) the calculated value at each node is placed above the forward rate, and (2) the coupon payment (and later the net settlement payment on interest rate swaps) is placed to the right of the node. The bond values for Date 3 are calculated as follows:

$$\frac{3.25 + [(0.50 * 95.5274) + (0.50 * 97.9425)]}{1.065184} = 93.8664$$

$$\frac{3.25 + [(0.50 * 97.9425) + (0.50 * 99.6310)]}{1.043694} = 97.7650$$

$$\frac{3.25 + [(0.50 * 99.6310) + (0.50 * 100.7957)]}{1.029289} = 100.5193$$

$$\frac{3.25 + [(0.50 * 100.7957) + (0.50 * 101.5918)]}{1.019633} = 102.4327$$

The numerators are the sum of scheduled coupon payment of 3.25 and the expected values for the bond on Date 4, using the essential feature in this model that the probabilities are equal for the forward rate going up and down. This is then discounted by the forward rate prevailing each of the four possible Date 3 nodes.

Proceeding with backward induction, we repeat the process for Dates 2, 1, and 0. These are the calculations for Date 2:

$$\frac{3.25 + [(0.50 * 93.8664) + (0.50 * 97.7650)]}{1.051111} = 94.2485$$

$$\frac{3.25 + [(0.50 * 97.7650) + (0.50 * 100.5193)]}{1.034261} = 99.0003$$

$$\frac{3.25 + [(0.50 * 100.5193) + (0.50 * 102.4327)]}{1.022966} = 102.3748$$

These are for Date 1:

$$\frac{3.25 + [(0.50 * 92.2485) + (0.50 * 99.0003)]}{1.036326} = 96.3735$$

$$\frac{3.25 + [(0.50 * 99.0003) + (0.50 * 102.3748)]}{1.024350} = 101.4668$$

Finally, we find that the bond value on Date 0 is 101.1586:

$$\frac{3.25 + [(0.50 * 96.3735) + (0.50 * 101.4668)]}{1.010000} = 101.1586$$

Clearly, repetitive calculations such as these are perfect for an Excel spreadsheet.

I.2: Pathwise Valuation of a Default-Risk-Free Bond Using a Binomial Tree

Another method to get the Date-0 value for the 5-year, 3.25%, annual payment government bond is known as *pathwise valuation*. The idea is to calculate the value for the bond using each of the possible forward rate paths through the tree. There are 16 paths in the binomial tree shown in Exhibit I-1. One path culminates in a rate of 8.0842% on Date 4, four in a rate of 5.4190%, six of 3.6324%, four of 2.4349%, and one of 1.6322%. [Some readers might recognize Pascal's Triangle in the pattern of outcomes.] The Date-0 value of the bond is then calculated for each path of forward rates. Those results are then averaged, producing the bond value consistent with the assumptions behind the binomial tree.

Exhibit I-5 reports the 16 paths and the bond values for each path. The average of the 16 values is 101.1586, matching the result produced by backward induction. The values range from 93.5650 using the forward rates at the top of the binomial tree to 106.5837 at the bottom of the tree. A couple of examples of the calculations illustrate how the values are obtained for each path. First, consider Path 1:

$$\cfrac{\cfrac{\cfrac{\cfrac{\cfrac{103.25}{1.080842}+3.25}{1.065184}+3.25}{1.051111}+3.25}{1.036326}+3.25}{1.010000}=93.5650$$

This pattern is maintained in the spreadsheet that produces Exhibit I-5. The bond value for Date 5 (103.25) is discounted by

Exhibit I-5: Pathwise Valuation of a 5-Year, 3.25%, Annual Payment Bond

Path	Date 0	Date 1	Date 2	Date 3	Date 4	Bond Value
1	1.0000%	3.6326%	5.1111%	6.5184%	8.0842%	93.5650
2	1.0000%	3.6326%	5.1111%	6.5184%	5.4190%	95.6259
3	1.0000%	3.6326%	5.1111%	4.3694%	5.4190%	97.4039
4	1.0000%	3.6326%	5.1111%	4.3694%	3.6324%	98.8743
5	1.0000%	3.6326%	3.4261%	4.3694%	5.4190%	98.8877
6	1.0000%	3.6326%	3.4261%	4.3694%	3.6324%	100.3822
7	1.0000%	3.6326%	3.4261%	2.9289%	3.6324%	101.6565
8	1.0000%	3.6326%	3.4261%	2.9289%	2.4349%	102.7018
9	1.0000%	2.4350%	3.4261%	4.3694%	5.4190%	100.0062
10	1.0000%	2.4350%	3.4261%	4.3694%	3.6324%	101.5182
11	1.0000%	2.4350%	3.4261%	2.9289%	3.6324%	102.8074
12	1.0000%	2.4350%	3.4261%	2.9289%	2.4349%	103.8649
13	1.0000%	2.4350%	2.2966%	2.9289%	3.6324%	103.8723
14	1.0000%	2.4350%	2.2966%	2.9289%	2.4349%	104.9415
15	1.0000%	2.4350%	2.2966%	1.9633%	2.4349%	105.8460
16	1.0000%	2.4350%	2.2966%	1.9633%	1.6322%	106.5837
					Average	101.1586

the Date-4 forward rate and the coupon payment (3.25) is added. That sum is discounted by the Date-3 rate and the coupon payment is added, and so forth working back to Date 0. Here is Path 10:

$$\cfrac{\cfrac{\cfrac{\cfrac{\cfrac{103.25}{1.036324} + 3.25}{1.043694} + 3.25}{1.034261} + 3.25}{1.024350} + 3.25}{1.010000} = 101.5182$$

Pathwise valuation visualizes nicely the Monte Carlo simulations that are used in the XVA engines in practice. Rather than just 16 possible paths, a multitude (thousands) are drawn from a probability distribution and the value for each path is calculated. The average of that multitude of results is the Date-0 value. I believe it is instructive for us non-quants to see a simple example of the much more detailed and complex models used by the quants to calculate the XVA.

An important observation from these calculations is that the value of a default-risk-free government bond is independent of interest rate volatility. We get the same value for the bond using the discount factors, spot rates, and forward rates, which are bootstrapped from the underlying benchmark par curve without any reference to volatility, as we get from the binomial tree that assumes 20% volatility. This finding is generally believed to extend to risky corporate bonds as long as there are no embedded options. However, we will see in the next chapter that this does not hold once credit risk is brought into the valuation model that assumes a log-normal probability distribution for rates.

I.3: Recommendations for Readers

I have been using binomial trees to illustrate bond pricing in my fixed income markets courses for over twenty years. I have found that students benefit from the "hands on" process of building the spreadsheets. As this book is essentially a tutorial, I suggest that readers follow along and replicate the Exhibits. I have seen students do wonderful things with color — the forward rates in one color, the coupon and principal payments to the right of the nodes in another color, and the calculated values in a third.

Here are some specific suggestions:

- Leave yourself plenty of room in the spreadsheet. For example, I have an empty column between the Dates and place the forward rates six cells apart. That is useful in debugging the spreadsheet because when you click on a calculated value, the pattern for the cells should be the same.
- Simplify the expected value in the numerator — it's easier to divide the sum by two than multiply each by 0.50. For instance, my equation for the Date-0 value in Exhibit I-4 is:

$$\frac{3.25 + (96.3735 + 101.4668)/2}{1.010000} = 101.1586$$

- Always link to the cells — only the forward rates in the tree need to be typed in.
- Place the coupon rate outside the tree and link to it. That way you can quickly change the coupon rate to find that a 5-year, 2.25%, annual payment bond value has a Date-0 value of 96.5242. If it's a zero-coupon bond, its price is 86.0968.

I have written study questions and answers for each chapter for readers who do plan to play along with their spreadsheets. Some new material is introduced in the Q&A sections. For instance, floating-rate notes having an interest rate cap are covered in the main text of Chapter III, whereas there is a question on floaters having an interest rate floor. Callable bonds are in the main text of Chapter IV; putable bonds are in a question. In Chapter V, the discussion in the text is on valuing an individual interest rate swap. The more complex (and realistic) problem of valuing a portfolio of swaps is dealt with in a question. Chapter VII works with inverse (bull) floaters and bear floaters in the main text and the study question combines them into a novel "bear to bull transformer" structured note. Therefore, readers who do not plan to replicate the Exhibits are still encouraged to read the Q&A.

Exhibit I-6: Valuation of a 5-Year, 1.50%, Annual Payment Bond Using Backward Induction

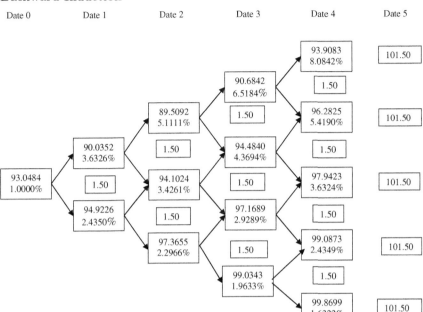

I.4: Study Questions

(A) Calculate the Date-0 value for a 5-year, 1.50%, annual payment default-risk-free government bond using backward induction and the binomial tree for 20% volatility presented in Exhibit I-1.

(B) Calculate the Date-0 value of the same bond using pathwise valuation.

I.5: Answers to the Study Questions

(A) First, use the discount factors (or the spot or forward rates) to determine that our target for the bond value using the binomial tree is 93.0484 (per 100 of par value).

$$(1.50 * 0.990099) + (1.50 * 0.960978) + (1.50 * 0.928023)$$

$$+ (1.50 * 0.894344) + (101.50 * 0.860968) = 93.0484$$

Exhibit I-7: Pathwise Valuation of a 5-Year, 1.50%, Annual Payment Bond

Path	Date 0	Date 1	Date 2	Date 3	Date 4	Bond Value
1	1.0000%	3.6326%	5.1111%	6.5184%	8.0842%	85.6949
2	1.0000%	3.6326%	5.1111%	6.5184%	5.4190%	87.7208
3	1.0000%	3.6326%	5.1111%	4.3694%	5.4190%	89.4388
4	1.0000%	3.6326%	5.1111%	4.3694%	3.6324%	90.8844
5	1.0000%	3.6326%	3.4261%	4.3694%	5.4190%	90.8484
6	1.0000%	3.6326%	3.4261%	4.3694%	3.6324%	92.3175
7	1.0000%	3.6326%	3.4261%	2.9289%	3.6324%	93.5493
8	1.0000%	3.6326%	3.4261%	2.9289%	2.4349%	94.5769
9	1.0000%	2.4350%	3.4261%	4.3694%	5.4190%	91.8932
10	1.0000%	2.4350%	3.4261%	4.3694%	3.6324%	93.3795
11	1.0000%	2.4350%	3.4261%	2.9289%	3.6324%	94.6257
12	1.0000%	2.4350%	3.4261%	2.9289%	2.4349%	95.6652
13	1.0000%	2.4350%	2.2966%	2.9289%	3.6324%	95.6381
14	1.0000%	2.4350%	2.2966%	2.9289%	2.4349%	96.6891
15	1.0000%	2.4350%	2.2966%	1.9633%	2.4349%	97.5636
16	1.0000%	2.4350%	2.2966%	1.9633%	1.6322%	98.2888
					Average	93.0484

Exhibit I-6 displays the binomial tree that obtains the same result.

(B) Exhibit I-7 demonstrates that the average of the 16 paths gives the same value of 93.0484 for 5-year, 1.50%, annual payment default-risk-free government bond. These are the calculations for Paths 4 and 13:

$$\cfrac{\cfrac{\cfrac{\cfrac{\cfrac{101.50}{1.036324} + 1.50}{1.043694} + 1.50}{1.051111} + 1.50}{1.036326} + 1.50}{1.010000} = 90.8844$$

$$\cfrac{\cfrac{\cfrac{\cfrac{\cfrac{101.50}{1.036324} + 1.50}{1.029289} + 1.50}{1.022966} + 1.50}{1.024350} + 1.50}{1.010000} = 95.6381$$

Chapter II

Valuing Traditional Fixed-Rate Corporate Bonds

This chapter addresses the valuation of a traditional fixed-rate corporate bond that does not have an embedded call or put option. The classic method to value the bond is discounted cash flow (DCF) analysis. Each scheduled coupon and principal payment is discounted back to Date 0 using a *spot* (or zero-coupon) rate that matches the time until the receipt of the cash flow and that reflects the investor's required rate of return given the risk. For an N-period bond making N evenly-spaced coupon payments (PMT) and having the redemption of principal (FV) entirely at maturity, the price of the bond (PV) depends on the sequence of spot rates $(Z_1, Z_2, \ldots, Z_N)$:

$$PV = \frac{PMT}{(1+Z_1)^1} + \frac{PMT}{(1+Z_2)^2} + \cdots + \frac{PMT+FV}{(1+Z_N)^N} \qquad (1)$$

Often a single discount rate, known as the *yield to maturity* (Y), is used in lieu of the sequence of spot rates:

$$PV = \frac{PMT}{(1+Y)^1} + \frac{PMT}{(1+Y)^2} + \cdots + \frac{PMT+FV}{(1+Y)^N} \qquad (2)$$

This yield to maturity is the internal rate of return on the cash flows, the uniform discount rate such that the present value of the coupon and principal payments equals the price. This yield can be interpreted as a "weighted average" of the spot rates with most of the weight on the final cash flow as it includes the principal.

The yield to maturity on a corporate bond is commonly separated for analysis into a benchmark yield, typically on a government bond, and a spread over (or, sometimes as with federal tax-exempt municipal bonds in the U.S, under) the benchmark. The benchmark bond yield itself is separated into the expected real rate of return and the expected inflation rate. To the extent that investors are risk-averse, there might also be additional compensation for the uncertainty regarding the inflation rate and, subsequently, the real rate of return. In general, the benchmark yield captures *macroeconomic* factors (for instance, the business cycle, monetary and fiscal policy, foreign exchange rates), and the spread over the benchmark captures *microeconomic* factors that are specific to the bond issuer and the issue itself. Those factors are the credit risk as measured by the expected loss due to default, liquidity and taxation. There might also be a component for compensation to risk-averse investors for the uncertainty regarding the expected loss arising from issuer default and future liquidity and tax problems. The salient aspect of DCF bond valuation is that the discount rates are adjusted for risk. This is pictured in Exhibit II-1.

An alternative to DCF valuation is XVA analysis. The bond price is its value assuming no default, denoted VND, minus a series of valuation adjustments collectively known as the XVA. The VND corresponds to the benchmark yield in DCF analysis and the XVA to the factors that comprise the spread. The XVA for bonds include the CVA (credit valuation adjustment), LVA (liquidity valuation adjustment), and TVA (taxation valuation adjustment). From the perspective of the investor, for whom the bond is an asset, the value in general is summarized as:

$$\text{Value}^{\text{ASSET}} = \text{VND} - \text{XVA} \qquad (3)$$

This decomposition allows for separate analysis and modeling of the credit, liquidity, and taxation effects on the differences between government benchmark bonds and corporate securities. For example,

Exhibit II-1: Components of a Corporate Bond Yield

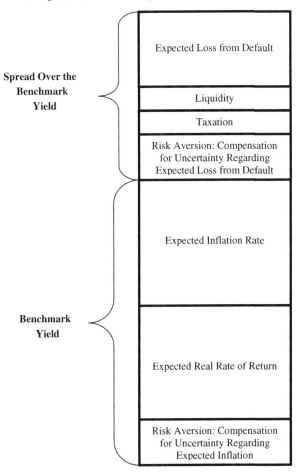

government bonds typically are more liquid than corporate bonds due to greater supply arising from the need to finance budget deficits and to greater demand because institutional investors are not precluded from holding benchmark securities, whereas they might have limitations on holding risky corporate bonds. Also, the presumed absence of credit risk and standardized features minimizes the time and cost to assess value, thereby facilitating trading and use as collateral. In some cases, government bonds have preferential tax treatment. For instance, interest income on U.S. Treasuries is exempt from taxation on the state and local levels, whereas on corporate bonds interest income is fully taxable.

The focus of this introduction to valuation using XVA is on the implications of credit risk and the expected loss due to default. Therefore, LVA and TVA going forward are neglected. By assumption, the benchmark bonds and the corporate bond under consideration have the same liquidity and taxation, so no further adjustment is needed. They differ only with regard to credit risk. Also, investors are assumed to be risk-neutral so that additional compensation is not needed for uncertainty regarding expected losses on the corporate bond. An alternative rationale for this simplification is to assume that, while differences in liquidity and taxation are factors in valuation, their impact is subsumed in the credit risk assumptions, along with any compensation for investor risk aversion.

With the simplifying assumption to neglect liquidity, taxation, and risk aversion, equation (3) becomes:

$$\text{Value}^{\text{ASSET}} = \text{VND} - \text{CVA} \tag{4}$$

CVA captures the default risk (and possibly the neglected effects) in present value terms. The spread over the benchmark bond yield captures the default risk in terms of annual basis points. The key point is that the value of the bond should be the same for each methodology.

Another of the XVA is used to value the bond from the perspective of the issuer. The DVA (debit, or debt, valuation adjustment) is the credit risk from the perspective of the issuer. The fair value of the liability is the VND minus DVA:

$$\text{Value}^{\text{LIABILITY}} = -(\text{VND} - \text{DVA}) = -\text{VND} + \text{DVA} \tag{5}$$

The minus sign in front of (VND – DVA) indicates that the security is a liability. In principle, CVA equals DVA. They differ only in perspective: CVA is the credit risk facing the bond investor and DVA is the credit risk viewed by the entity that issues the security.

Combining (4) and (5) reveals an important identity about financial assets and liabilities:

$$\text{Value}^{\text{ASSET}} + \text{Value}^{\text{LIABILITY}}$$

$$= \text{VND} - \text{CVA} - \text{VND} + \text{DVA} = 0 \tag{6}$$

This is often expressed in academic articles as the securities existing
in *zero net supply*. The idea is that the fair value of a bond is the
same amount (in absolute value) whether viewed by the investor or
the issuer. Financial assets equal financial liabilities when they are
aggregated, at least in terms of the economics of the transactions.
Accounting rules sometimes lead to a different result, for instance,
if investors are required to carry their assets at market value and
issuers are allowed to carry their liabilities at book value.

The VND on a traditional fixed-rate bond can be calculated
directly using the benchmark bond discount factors (or spot and forward rates) as in Chapter I. It also can be calculated using a binomial
tree because the forward rates are applicable to the underlying risk-
free benchmark bonds. The CVA depends on the credit risk of the
issuer of the bond. The credit risk is captured by the *probability of
default* for each time period and the *recovery rate* if default occurs.
The *expected exposure* is a key element in the CVA calculation. It is
the expected value of the asset on each future date if it were risk-
free — this is where the binomial tree model and the probabilities of
attaining particular values at the various nodes come into play. The
remaining terms in the CVA are the discount factors that are used
to state the credit risk as a present value.

In general, the CVA is the sum of the products of the four terms
for each date[1]:

$$\text{CVA} = \sum_{t=1}^{T}(\text{Expected Exposure}_t) * (1 - \text{Recovery Rate}_t)$$

$$* (\text{Probability of Default}_{t-1,t}) * (\text{Discount Factor}_t) \tag{7}$$

The $(1-$ Recovery Rate$_t)$ term is known as the *loss severity*. The
product of the expected exposure and the loss severity is the *loss
given default* (LGD). The assumed probability of default (POD) is

for the time period between Date t-1 and Date t, conditional on no prior default. Implicit in this formulation for CVA is the assumption that the event of default can occur at any time between Date t-1 and Date t; the financial impact, however, is experienced only on Date t. That is when the loss is realized and the recovery is (instantaneously) made. The discount factors for the T dates are bootstrapped from the underlying benchmark bonds as described in the Appendix.

We need to distinguish *risk-neutral* probabilities of default and *actual* (or historical) default probabilities in credit risk models. Here "risk-neutral" follows the usage of the term in option pricing. In the risk-neutral option pricing methodology, the expected value for the option payoffs is discounted using the risk-free interest rate. The key point is that in taking the expected value, the risk-neutral probabilities associated with the payoffs are used and not the actual probabilities (even if they are known). The same idea applies to valuing risky corporate bonds.

Suppose a 1-year, 4%, annual payment, corporate bond is priced at par value. At the same time, a 1-year, 3%, annual payment government bond is also priced at par value. The credit spread is 100 basis points. Next suppose that a credit rating agency has collected an extensive data set on the historical default experience for 1-year corporate bonds issued by firms having the same business profile. It is observed that 99% of the bonds survive and make the full coupon and principal payment at maturity. Just 1% of the bonds default, resulting in an average recovery of 50 per 100 of par value. Based on this data, the actual default probability for the corporate bond can reasonably be assumed to be 1%.

If the actual default probability is used and the assumed recovery is 50, the expected future value for the corporate bond is 103.46:$(104 * 0.99) + (50 * 0.01) = 103.46$. Discounting that at the risk-free rate of 3% gives a present value of 100.4466: $103.46/1.03 = 100.4466$. That overstates the value of the bond, which is observed to be 100. Denote the risk-neutral default probability to be P^* so that the probability of survival is $1 - P^*$. Given that the corporate bond is priced at 100, $P^* = 1.85\%$. This is found as the solution to P^* in this equation:

$$100 = \frac{[104 \times (1 - P^*)] + [50 \times P^*]}{1.03}$$

The key point is that actual (or historical) default probabilities neglect the default risk premium. In valuing comparable risky bonds, for instance, ones having a different coupon rate, the risk-neutral default probability of 1.85% should be used in the model, not the actual probability of 1%.[2]

Some examples of the calculation of VND and CVA are useful to illustrate the implications of explicit modeling of credit risk in the valuation of a traditional fixed-rate bond.

II.1: The CVA and DVA on a Newly Issued 3.50% Fixed-Rate Corporate Bond

Consider first a newly issued 5-year, 3.50%, annual payment corporate bond. Exhibit II-2 includes the binomial forward rate tree that is used to value the bond — it is the same tree used in Chapter I to value the default-risk-free government bond. The same backward induction method is used to get the VND for the risky corporate bond. The VND on Date 0 is 102.3172 (per 100 of par value). This is what the value of the corporate bond would be if there was no risk of default.

Exhibit II-3 shows the credit risk table used to get the CVA and DVA on the corporate bond. It is assumed that the (risk-neutral) *conditional* probability of default by the corporation is 0.82096% for each date — actually for this example that probability is determined by trial-and-error search to get the result that the initial fair value of the bond rounds to 100.0000. The recovery rate is assumed to be constant at 40%; therefore, the loss severity is 60%. The discount factors are from Exhibit I-3 and are based on the risk-free benchmark bonds.

By assumption, the probability of default (POD) on Date 0 is zero. The POD for the first year is 0.82096%. Therefore, the probability of survival to Date 1 is 99.17904% [= 100% − 0.82096%]. The POD for the second year, conditional on no prior default, is 0.81422%

Exhibit II-2: Valuation of a Newly Issued, 3.50%, 5-Year, Annual Coupon Payment Corporate Bond for 20% Volatility

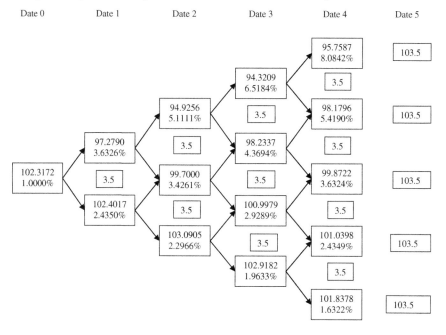

Exhibit II-3: Credit Risk Model for the Newly Issued, 3.50%, 5-Year, Annual Coupon Payment Corporate Bond

Credit Risk Parameters: 0.82096% Conditional Probability of Default, 40% Recovery Rate

Date	Expected Exposure	LGD	POD	Discount Factor	CVA
1	103.3404	62.0042	0.82096%	0.990099	0.5040
2	102.8540	61.7124	0.81422%	0.960978	0.4829
3	102.8667	61.7200	0.80754%	0.928023	0.4625
4	103.1067	61.8640	0.80091%	0.894344	0.4431
5	103.5000	62.1000	0.79433%	0.860968	0.4247
			4.03795%		2.3172

Fair Value = 102.3172 − 2.3172 = 100.0000

[= 99.17904% ∗ 0.82096%] and the probability of survival to Date 2 is 98.36482% [= 99.17904% − 0.81422%], and so forth. For each year, the sum of the probabilities of default and survival equal the probability of entering that year without prior default. This is shown in Exhibit II-4. Notice that the cumulative probability of default on this bond is 4.03795%, the sum of the default probabilities for each year.

Exhibit II-4: The Probabilities of Default and Survival

Date	Probability of Default	Probability of Survival	Sum
1	0.82096%	99.17904%	100.00000%
2	0.81422%	98.36482%	99.17904%
3	0.80754%	97.55728%	98.36482%
4	0.80091%	96.75638%	97.55728%
5	0.79433%	95.96205%	96.75638%
	4.03795%		

That corresponds to the 95.96205% probability of survival on Date 5: $4.03795\% + 95.96205\% = 100.00000\%$.

In Exhibit II-3 the expected exposure to default loss for each date uses the bond values that are calculated in the tree, the probabilities first shown in Exhibit I-1 for arrival at each particular node, and the scheduled coupon payment. These are the calculations:

Date 1: $[(0.50 * 97.2790) + (0.50 * 102.4017)] + 3.5 = 103.3404$

Date 2: $[(0.25 * 94.9256) + (0.50 * 99.7000)$
$+ (0.25 * 103.0905)] + 3.5 = 102.8540$

Date 3: $[(0.125 * 94.3209) + (0.375 * 98.2337) + (0.375 * 100.9979)$
$+ (0.125 * 102.9182)] + 3.5 = 102.8667$

Date 4: $[(0.0625 * 95.7587) + (0.2500 * 98.1796)$
$+ (0.3750 * 99.8722) + (0.2500 * 101.0398)$
$+ (0.0625 * 101.8378)] + 3.50 = 103.1067$

The expected exposure for Date 5 is obviously 103.5000, the principal redemption plus the final coupon.

The loss given default (LGD) is the expected exposure multiplied by the loss severity, which is one minus the recovery rate. For Date 4 the LGD is 61.8640[$= 103.1067 * (1 - 0.40)$]. The CVA for each date is the LGD times the POD times the Discount Factor. For Date 4 the CVA is 0.4431 (per 100 of par value): $61.8640*0.0080091*0.894344 = 0.4431$. The sum of the CVAs for the various dates is the overall CVA, 2.3172 (per 100 of par value). This also is the DVA applicable to the issuer of the bond. This bond is priced at par value at issuance: $102.3172 - 2.3172 = 100.0000$.

Given the assumptions, the CVA of 2.3172 summarizes the credit risk on the bond in terms of present value as of Date 0. The credit risk also can be summarized by the spread over the yield on the benchmark bond having the same time to maturity. This 3.50%, 5-year corporate bond priced at par value has a yield to maturity of 3.50% and the 5-year bond on the benchmark par curve yields 3.00%. Therefore, the annual credit spread is 50 basis points: $0.0350 - 0.0300 = 0.0050$. This spread over the maturity-matching government bond yield is sometimes called the *G-spread*.

Another version for the annual compensation for credit risk is the *Z-spread* (from "zero-volatility"), which is the uniform mark-up over the benchmark spot rates such that the present value of the coupon and principal payments equals the bond price. It is the solution for Z in this expression, found by trial-and-error search:

$$100.0000 = \frac{3.5}{(1 + 0.010000 + Z)^1} + \frac{3.5}{(1 + 0.020101 + Z)^2}$$

$$+ \frac{3.5}{(1 + 0.025212 + Z)^3} + \frac{3.5}{(1 + 0.028310 + Z)^4}$$

$$+ \frac{103.5}{(1 + 0.030392 + Z)^5}, \quad Z = 0.005065$$

The spot rates are taken from Exhibit I-3. The Z-spread (which is also called the *static spread*) for this bond is 50.65 basis points. The difference between the G-spread and the Z-spread becomes more significant with longer times to maturity and greater slope to the benchmark bond par curve. The difference is also more significant for debt securities that *amortize* the principal payments, for instance, a corporate bond having a sinking fund or a mortgage-backed bond given an assumed pace of homeowner prepayments.

When this 3.50%, annual coupon payment, 5-year corporate bond is issued at par value, the VND of 102.3172 and the CVA/DVA of 2.3172 do not appear on the balance sheet of the investor or the issuer. All that is recognized is the purchase and issuance price of 100.0000. Nevertheless, the VND and the CVA/DVA — and any ensuing changes in those variables — are important for risk management and investment analysis. If either the investor or the issuer were to hedge the interest rate or credit risk inherent in the corporate bond, those variables become very useful. Under financial accounting rules, to qualify for hedge accounting treatment the entity needs to designate the type of risk being hedged (for instance, sensitivity to a change in the benchmark yield or to a change in the credit risk) and to assess periodically the effectiveness of the hedge. Therefore, tracking ensuing changes in the VND and the CVA/DVA compared to changes in the value of the hedging instrument is an integral part of risk management. Even if the interest rate or credit risks to the bond were not being hedged, an analyst would want to understand (and be able to explain) the source of changes in the bond price and yield. It is constructive to frame the analysis in the context of changes in the VND and CVA/DVA, as demonstrated in the next example.

II.2: The CVA and DVA on a Seasoned 3.50% Fixed-Rate Corporate Bond

Next consider a *seasoned*, 5-year, 3.50%, annual payment corporate bond. Assume that the bond was issued at par value two years ago as a 7-year offering. Now, on Date 0, the bond needs to be valued by both the investor and the issuer to produce financial statements. How the result is reported depends on the information that is available to get the current fair value. Under current accounting guidelines, there are three possibilities: (1) market prices on trades in the same security (referred to as "Level 1" inputs), (2) observable inputs to a valuation model such as market prices on trades for similar but not identical securities ("Level 2" inputs), and (3) unobservable inputs to a valuation model such as internal management cash flow estimates ("Level 3" inputs). The binomial tree model and the calculation of CVA/DVA are useful to illustrate these alternatives.

First, suppose that this corporate bond is illiquid and that there are no data on recent trades for the security. Therefore, the bond needs to be "marked to model" based on *unobserved* inputs. The derived value is included in the entity's Level 3 bucket of assets. Suppose that a fixed-income analyst estimates the conditional probability of default to be 1.75% and the recovery rate to be 35% for each year based on the available information regarding the issuer, perhaps including its status with the credit rating agencies (the current rating and whether it is on a watch list). These are assumed to apply to each date uniformly to keep the example simple but clearly the tabular calculation method is amenable to a *term structure* of default probabilities and recovery rates.

Exhibit II-5 displays the calculation of the VND and CVA, and the resulting fair value. The VND is 102.3172, the same as in

Exhibit II-5: Valuation of the Seasoned, 3.50%, 5-Year, Annual Coupon Payment Corporate Bond for 20% Volatility

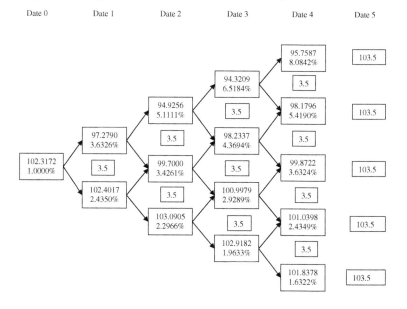

Credit Risk Parameters: 1.75% Conditional Probability of Default, 35% Recovery Rate

Date	Expected Exposure	LGD	POD	Discount Factor	CVA
1	103.3404	67.1712	1.75000%	0.990099	1.1639
2	102.8540	66.8551	1.71938%	0.960978	1.1046
3	102.8667	66.8634	1.68929%	0.928023	1.0482
4	103.1067	67.0194	1.65972%	0.894344	0.9948
5	103.5000	67.2750	1.63068%	0.860968	0.9445
			8.44906%		5.2560

Fair Value = 102.3172 – 5.2560 = 97.0612 (97.06117889)

Exhibit II-2 because the coupon rate and time to maturity are the same as the newly issued bond. The CVA is 5.2560, so the estimated fair value of the bond is 97.0612(=102.3172 − 5.2560). [The more precise fair value of 97.06117889 is used later in this chapter]. The bond trades at a discount below par value because, compared to the newly issued bond having the same coupon rate and time to maturity, the conditional annual probability of default (1.75% versus 0.82096%) and the loss severity (65% versus 60%) are higher. The cumulative probability of default is much higher as well (8.44906% versus 4.03795%). The greater degree of credit risk on this seasoned bond also is reflected in its yield to maturity of 4.1632%, found as the solution for Y in this expression:

$$97.0612 = \frac{3.5}{(1+Y)^1} + \frac{3.5}{(1+Y)^2} + \frac{3.5}{(1+Y)^3}$$
$$+ \frac{3.5}{(1+Y)^4} + \frac{103.5}{(1+Y)^5}, \quad Y = 0.041632$$

Given the benchmark yield of 3.00%, the credit spread is 116.32 basis points compared to 50 basis points on the newly issued bond.

Second, suppose that the seasoned corporate bond, while still not actively traded, can be valued by comparison to other bonds issued by the same or closely related companies. This is known as *matrix pricing* and is a good example of securities that are reported as Level 2 assets because the inputs to the valuation process — the prices and yields on the comparable bonds — are *observable*. In this method, the coupon rates and times to maturity on the other bonds, which by design pose the same degree of credit risk to the investor, are arrayed in the matrix. Then the presumed yield to maturity (or spread over the benchmark yield) on the illiquid bond is estimated via interpolation.

Suppose that as a result of the matrix pricing, the seasoned bond is estimated to have a yield to maturity of 4.1632%, or a spread of 116.32 basis points over the benchmark government bond. Based on this information, the price of the bond is estimated to be 97.0612. Given the VND for the bond of 102.3172, the CVA is estimated to be 5.2560. From this result for the CVA, the corresponding default probability can be obtained for a chosen recovery rate. As illustrated in Exhibit II-5, for a recovery rate of 35%, the conditional default probability is 1.75%. The CVA model can be used to calculate the corresponding default probability for other assumptions about the loss severity. For example, if the recovery rate is 40% (loss severity of 60%), the conditional default probability that produces a CVA of 5.2560 turns out to be 1.90136%, found by trial-and-error search. If the recovery rate is 30% (loss severity of 70%), the implied probability of default is 1.62095%. In general, for a given CVA, the default probability and loss severity are inversely related.

Third, suppose that the 3.50%, 5-year seasoned corporate bond is a liquid security, albeit not as frequently traded as the benchmark security, and that there are observed market prices. This is an example of an asset reported as a Level 1 fair value. Suppose that this market price is again 97.0612 and the yield to maturity is 4.1632%. As above, the implied probability of default for each year can be obtained for a particular assumption about the recovery rate.

Regardless of whether the seasoned corporate bond price is deemed to be a Level 1, 2, or 3 fair value for the purpose of financial reporting, the change in the CVA matters to the investor — and the equivalent change in the DVA matters to the issuer. Note that for Level 1 and Level 2 securities, the equality of CVA and DVA is reasonable as both the investor and issuer observe the same inputs. It could be a problem for Level 3 bonds that are marked to model because the investor and issuer perhaps could justifiably use different inputs to their valuation models.

In the spirit of an introduction to valuation issues using simplifying assumptions, suppose that on Date 0 the seasoned bond is priced at par value just before the release of the information that leads to the reassessment of its credit risk. Like the newly issued 3.50%, 5-year bond, its CVA is 2.3172 based on a conditional default probability of 0.82096% and a recovery rate of 40%. Then, after the release of the negative information or perhaps an unexpected downgrade in the bond's credit rating, the bond price drops to 97.0612. The change in the bond price is 2.9388 (= 100.0000 − 97.0612). Based on the revised default probability of 1.75% and the recovery rate of

35%, the new CVA is 5.2560. Notice that the change in the CVA is also 2.9388 (=5.2560 − 2.3172). The entire price event is credit-related because the VND remains unchanged at 102.3172, indicating no change in the macroeconomic factors that determine benchmark yields.

That the investor needs to write down the value of the corporate bond on Date 0 by 2.9388 per 100 of par value on its balance sheet is not controversial. In fact, to not do so would be suspect. However, it is not obvious if the change in value needs to flow through the income statement. Accounting rules allow the bond to be carried either in a trading account or as an available-for-sale (AFS) security. If the investor holds the bond in its trading account, the change in value flows through the income statement. Therefore, it impacts the widely watched earnings-per-share number before getting to the balance sheet, in particular to the component of shareholder's equity known as accumulated other comprehensive income (AOCI). If the investor designates the corporate bond to be an AFS asset, the change in value does not go through the income statement. Instead, it goes directly to AOCI without impacting earnings per share.

The corporation that issued the bond presumably has just experienced a significant negative event on Date 0 — the value of its bond fell by 2.9388%. The increase in the DVA reduces the market price of its debt liability. That "gain" to the bond issuer is indeed quite controversial, especially when it flows through the income statement as a source of "earnings" before "increasing" shareholder's equity in form of higher AOCI. Nevertheless, it does not make *economic* sense for bond investors to value the asset at 97.0612 and the issuer to value its liability at anything other than 97.0612, especially when those values are determined from market-traded prices or observable inputs. However, some *accounting* rules permit the bond issuer to choose between carrying a debt liability at fair value or at book value (unless the bond has been hedged with a derivative — then its reported value reflects the cumulative change in the specified interest rate or credit risk). A separate matter is how regulators (and investors in general) assess the "gain" associated with an increase in DVA. For instance, the Basel Committee on Banking Supervision has ruled that for measuring capital adequacy for commercial banks, "gains" resulting from higher DVA do not count as increases in Tier I equity.

II.3: The Impact of Volatility on Bond Valuation via Credit Risk

The assumed level of future interest rate volatility is critical to valuation using the binomial forward rate tree model. It is well known that volatility has a significant impact on option values, for instance, the embedded call option in a callable bond. Not so well known is that volatility also impacts credit risk via the expected exposure to default loss. Therefore, a change in the assumed level of volatility impacts the fair value of a traditional fixed-income bond having no embedded options through the CVA calculation. This is demonstrated in this section by comparing the results for 20% volatility to those produced by a new tree that reflects 10% volatility.

Exhibit II-6 displays a binomial forward rate tree consistent with the underlying par curve for annual coupon payment benchmark bonds and 10% volatility. As in Exhibit I-2, these bonds have coupon rates of 1.00%, 2.00%, 2.50%, 2.80%, and 3.00%, respectively, for times to maturity from one to five years and each bond is priced at par value. The tree is produced in the same manner as described in the Appendix. The implied forward rate is used to get trial rates, which then are raised or lowered until a value for the benchmark bond is produced that rounds to 100.0000. The calibration maintains the proportionality factor (which for 10% volatility is 1.221403) between adjoining rates because volatility is assumed to be constant over time. Those projected rates (rounded to four digits) are set and the process moves out to the next benchmark bond and is repeated.

As expected, the range of rates for each date is narrower than in Exhibit I-1 for 20% volatility. The range for the rates for Date 4 is from 2.5563% to just 5.6892% for 10% volatility. When the volatility assumption is 20%, the rates go from 1.6322% to 8.0842%. The

Exhibit II-6: Binomial Forward Rate Tree Using 10% Volatility

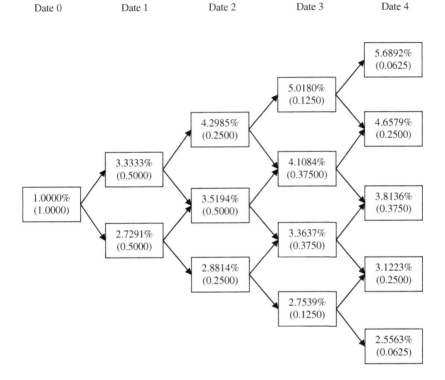

impact of changing the volatility assumption on the 3.50%, 5-year, seasoned corporate bond is shown in Exhibit II-7. For 20% volatility, the fair value for the bond is 97.0612, based on a VND of 102.3172 and CVA of 5.2560. Now for 10% volatility, the fair value is 97.0606, a small difference but a difference nonetheless. The VND remains 102.3172, indicating that the valuation of a risk-free bond government is *independent* of the volatility assumption. The CVA in Exhibit II-7 is 5.2566. The lesser degree of interest rate volatility reduces the bond value slightly because the credit risk is slightly higher, as measured by the CVA.

Even though the assumed probability of default and the recovery rate are the same in Exhibits II-5 and II-7, the expected exposure (and, therefore, the loss given default) is a bit higher when the volatility is lowered from 20% to 10%. Intuitively, higher volatility

Exhibit II-7: Valuation of the Seasoned, 3.50%, 5-Year, Annual Coupon Payment Corporate Bond Using 10% Volatility

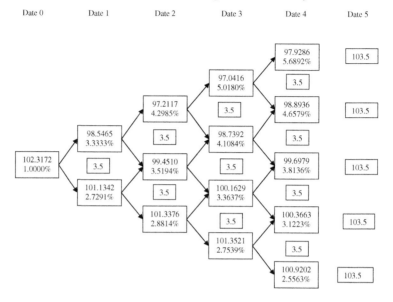

Credit Risk Parameters: 1.75% Conditional Probability of Default, 35% Recovery Rate

Date	Expected Exposure	LGD	POD	Discount Factor	CVA
1	103.3404	67.1712	1.75000%	0.990099	1.1639
2	102.8628	66.8608	1.71938%	0.960978	1.1047
3	102.8875	66.8769	1.68929%	0.928023	1.0484
4	103.1297	67.0343	1.65972%	0.894344	0.9950
5	103.5000	67.2750	1.63068%	0.860968	0.9445
			8.44906%		5.2566

Fair Value = 102.3172 – 5.2566 = 97.0606

leads to higher rates and lower bond values at the top of the tree. Hence, there is less value to be lost if the issuer were to default. More technically, the result arises from the assumption of a log-normal probability distribution for interest rates, as discussed in the Appendix.

That interest rate volatility has an effect, albeit minor, on the credit risk and fair value of a bond having no embedded options is a novel finding. Usually the volatility effect is demonstrated only on callable and putable bonds in fixed-income textbooks.

II.4: Duration and Convexity of a Traditional Fixed-Rate Bond

Duration and convexity are statistics that are commonly used to measure the price sensitivity of debt securities. There are variations but in general they measure the change in market value, either as a percentage or in terms of currency units, given a change in some measure of the level of interest rates. Duration is the first-order effect, essentially the first derivative of the relationship between market value and the interest rate; convexity is the second-order effect, the second derivative of the relationship.

There are two general types of price sensitivity statistics — *yield* duration and convexity, and *curve* duration and convexity. Yield duration and convexity estimate the price sensitivity to a change in the bond's own yield to maturity; curve duration and convexity estimate the sensitivity to a change in a benchmark bond yield curve. This section illustrates the sensitivity to a shift in the benchmark bond par curve because it is calculable using the binomial forward rate tree model. These statistics are commonly called *effective duration* and *effective convexity*.

It is instructive to see the numerical differences between yield and curve duration and convexity on the seasoned 3.50%, 5-year, annual payment, corporate bond that has a fair value of 97.0612 (per 100 of par value) and a yield to maturity of 4.1632%. A formula to calculate the modified duration statistic for a fixed-rate bond is:

$$\text{Modified Duration} = \frac{1}{y} - \frac{1 + \dfrac{N * (c - y)}{1 + y}}{c * [(1 + y)^N - 1] + y} \tag{8}$$

In this equation y is the yield to maturity per period, c is the coupon rate per period, and N is the number of periods to maturity. This formula applies to a coupon payment date so that N is an integer and there is no accrued interest.[3] Substituting $y = 0.041632$, $c = 0.0350$, and $N = 5$ for this annual payment bond obtains a modified duration of 4.4808.[4]

$$\frac{1}{0.041632} - \frac{1 + \dfrac{5 * (0.0350 - 0.041632)}{1.041632}}{0.0350 * [(1.041632)^5 - 1] + 0.041632} = 4.4808$$

A formula to calculate the convexity statistic for the bond using the same inputs is[5]:

$$\text{Convexity} = \frac{\begin{bmatrix} 2 * c * (1+y)^2 * \left((1+y)^N - \dfrac{1+y+(y*N)}{1+y} \right) \end{bmatrix} + \left[N * (N+1) * y^2 * (y-c) \right]}{y^2 * (1+y)^2 * (c * [(1+y)^N - 1] + y)} \tag{9}$$

This bond has a convexity of 25.2097.

$$\frac{\begin{bmatrix} 2 * 0.0350 * (1.041632)^2 * \left((1.041632)^5 - \dfrac{1.041632 + (0.041632 * 5)}{1.041632} \right) \end{bmatrix} + [5 * (5+1) * (0.041632)^2 * (0.041632 - 0.0350)]}{(0.041632)^2 * (1.041632)^2 * (0.0350 * [(1.041632)^5 - 1] + 0.041632)}$$

$$= 25.2097$$

[Note that in practice, that is, on Bloomberg and other data vendors, the convexity statistic often is divided by 100 and would be reported to be 0.252097.]

These risk statistics for the corporate bond — a modified duration of 4.4808 and a convexity of 25.2097 — pertain to a change in the bond's own yield to maturity and are the *yield* duration and convexity. A common application is to estimate the percentage change in the price of the bond (%ΔPrice) for a given change in the yield (ΔYield):

$$\%\Delta\text{Price} \approx -\text{Modified Duration} * \Delta\text{Yield}$$
$$+ [1/2 * \text{Convexity} * (\Delta\text{Yield})^2] \tag{10}$$

The term in brackets is known as the *convexity adjustment* to the estimate provided by duration alone. For example, if the yield to maturity on this bond were to go up instantaneously by 50 basis points from 4.1632% to 4.6632%, the estimated drop in the price is 2.2089%.

$$\%\Delta\text{Price} \approx -4.4808 * 0.0050 + [1/2 * 25.2097 * (0.0050)^2]$$
$$= -0.022089$$

This change in the yield to maturity could be due to an increase in the benchmark bond yield, arising from an increase in the expected inflation or real rate, or an increase in the credit spread, or in some combination of factors.

Curve duration and convexity estimate the impact on the price of the bond following a parallel ("shape-preserving") shift to the benchmark bond *yield curve*, usually the par curve although in principle the shift could be to the spot or forward curve. Separate analysis is needed to estimate the impact of a change in credit risk. While most applicable to interest rate derivatives, floating-rate notes, and bonds having embedded options (because on these there is no well-defined yield-to-maturity statistic), curve duration and convexity statistics also can be calculated for a traditional fixed-rate bond. The idea is to raise and lower the benchmark bond par curve and calculate anew the fair values by subtracting the CVA (assuming the same credit risk parameters) from the VND, which is based on the revised binomial tree.

Exhibit II-8 shows the new benchmark bond par curve and the new discount factors after the original par curve in Exhibit I-2 is "bumped" up by five basis points. The benchmark bonds are still priced at par value, but the coupon rates and, therefore, the yields to maturity all are five basis points higher. Next, the new binomial tree, displayed in Exhibit II-9, is derived following the procedures outlined in the Appendix. Note that in the middle of the tree, the 1-year projected forward rates go up by about five basis points compared to Exhibit I-1. However, at the top of the tree the rates go up by more than five basis points — and at the bottom the rates go up by less.

Exhibit II-8: Underlying Risk-Free Benchmark Coupon Rates, Prices, and Discount Factors after a 5-Basis-Point Upward Shift in the Benchmark Par Curve

Date	Coupon Rate	Price	Discount Factor
1	1.05%	100	0.989609
2	2.05%	100	0.960032
3	2.55%	100	0.926654
4	2.85%	100	0.892587
5	3.05%	100	0.858854

Exhibit II-9: Binomial Forward Rate Tree for 20% Volatility After a 5-Basis-Point Upward Shift in the Benchmark Par Curve

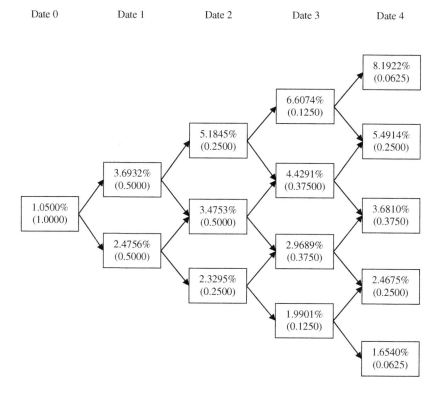

Exhibit II-10: Underlying Risk-Free Benchmark Coupon Rates, Prices, and Discount Factors after a 5-Basis-Point Downward Shift in the Benchmark Par Curve

Date	Coupon Rate	Price	Discount Factor
1	0.95%	100	0.990589
2	1.95%	100	0.961926
3	2.45%	100	0.929393
4	2.75%	100	0.896105
5	2.95%	100	0.863088

That is due to the log-normality assumption used to construct the binomial tree, as discussed in the Appendix.

Exhibit II-10 shows the new coupon rates and the discount factors after the original par curve is shifted down by five basis points. Exhibit II-11 displays the corresponding binomial tree — all the

Exhibit II-11: Binomial Forward Rate Tree for 20% Volatility After a 5-Basis-Point Downward Shift in the Benchmark Par Curve

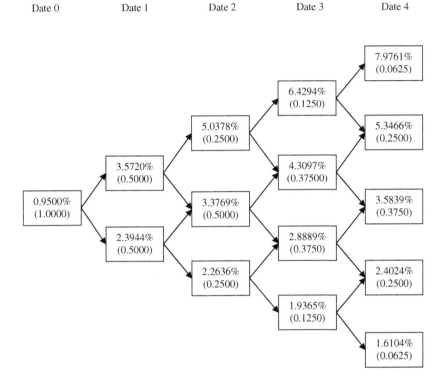

| Date 0 | Date 1 | Date 2 | Date 3 | Date 4 |

1-year rates go down but those at the top of the tree go down by more than those at the bottom. As with all the trees in this book, the ones portrayed are not necessarily unique because they depend on decisions made about rounding. Therefore, more than one tree might produce the desired price for the benchmark bond rounded to the chosen degree of precision, here four decimals (100.0000). However, any differences in the projected 1-year forward rates are only in the fourth decimal and will not change any of the qualitative observations and conclusions.

The valuation for the 5-year, 3.50% seasoned corporate bond following the upward shift is shown in Exhibit II-12. The VND drops from 102.3172 to 102.0825, a change of 0.2347 per 100 of par value. However, the change in the fair value is only 0.2222, a reduction from

Exhibit II-12: Valuation of the Seasoned, 3.50%, 5-Year, Corporate Bond After a 5-Basis-Point Upward Shift in the Benchmark Par Curve

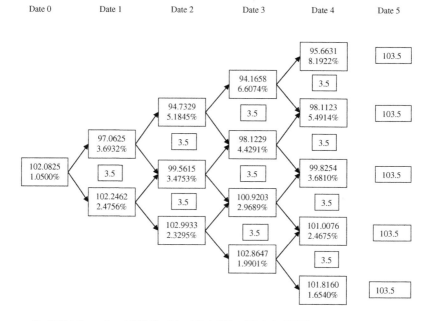

| Date 0 | Date 1 | Date 2 | Date 3 | Date 4 | Date 5 |

Credit Risk Parameters: 1.75% Conditional Probability of Default, 35% Recovery Rate

Date	Expected Exposure	LGD	POD	Discount Factor	CVA
1	103.1543	67.0503	1.75000%	0.989609	1.1612
2	102.7123	66.7630	1.71938%	0.960032	1.1020
3	102.7700	66.8005	1.68929%	0.926654	1.0457
4	103.0570	66.9870	1.65972%	0.892587	0.9924
5	103.5000	67.2750	1.63068%	0.858854	0.9442
					5.2435

Fair Value = 102.0825 – 5.2435 = 96.8390 (96.83901004)

97.0612 to 96.8390. A smaller change in the fair value than the VND also appears in Exhibit II-13, showing the valuation after the 5-basis-point downward shift in the benchmark bond par curve. The VND goes up from 102.3172 to 102.5526, an increase of 0.2354, whereas the fair value moves up by only 0.2228, from 97.0612 to 97.2840. Note that the greater price changes (in absolute value) when benchmark rates go down than when rates go up is a reflection of convexity — that is, that the relationship between the bond price and benchmark yield is not linear.

Exhibit II-13: Valuation of the Seasoned, 3.50%, 5-Year, Corporate Bond After a 5-Basis-Point Downward Shift in the Benchmark Par Curve

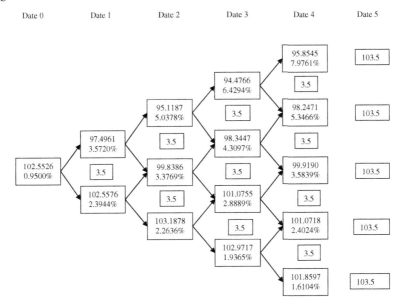

Credit Risk Parameters: 1.75% Conditional Probability of Default, 35% Recovery Rate

Date	Expected Exposure	LGD	POD	Discount Factor	CVA
1	103.5269	67.2925	1.75000%	0.990589	1.1665
2	102.9960	66.9474	1.71938%	0.961926	1.1073
3	102.9636	66.9263	1.68929%	0.929393	1.0508
4	103.1565	67.0517	1.65972%	0.896105	0.9973
5	103.5000	67.2750	1.63068%	0.863088	0.9468
					5.2586

Fair Value = 102.5526 – 5.2586 = 97.2840 (97.28397531)

The reason why the change in fair value is less than the change in the VND than in the fair value of the corporate bond is that the valuation of credit risk has an offsetting effect. When the benchmark yield curve is bumped up, the bond values throughout the binomial tree go down, thereby reducing the expected exposure to default loss and reducing the CVA. The original adjustment for credit risk is 5.2560, whereas it is 5.2435 in Exhibit II-12. When the yield curve is shifted downward, bond values go up and raise the expected exposure. In Exhibit II-13, the CVA increases to 5.2686.

This change in the valuation of credit risk occurs even though the key parameters — the assumed probability of default and the recovery rate — are unchanged.

The observation that the price sensitivity of the fair value is less than the VND contributes to explaining why in practice corporate bond prices typically are less volatile than Treasuries. One explanation is mathematical — corporate bonds have higher yields to maturity than otherwise comparable government bonds (meaning the same coupon rate, same payment frequency, same time to maturity) and it is well known that the duration statistic is inversely related to the yield. Another explanation is more market-driven—international capital flows impact the demand and supply of Treasuries more than corporate bonds because of greater liquidity. Another factor, which is observed here, is credit risk to the investor: lower (higher) benchmark rates raise (lower) corporate bond prices and increase (decrease) potential losses if there is a default. The change in the CVA offsets and reduces the change in the VND.

The effective duration and convexity statistics measure the price sensitivity using numerical methods to estimate the first and second derivatives of the relationship between the bond price and the interest rate level. These are the formulas:

$$\text{Effective Duration} = \frac{(MV_-) - (MV_+)}{2 * \Delta \text{Curve} * (MV_0)} \quad (11)$$

$$\text{Effective Convexity} = \frac{[(MV_-) + (MV_+)] - [2 * (MV_0)]}{(\Delta \text{Curve})^2 * (MV_0)} \quad (12)$$

$MV-$ and MV_+ are the new market values (or, as used here, the new fair values) after the benchmark bond yield curve is shifted down and up, respectively, and MV_0 is the original market value. $\Delta Curve$ is the change in the benchmark bond yield curve expressed as a decimal.

The calculations of effective duration and, especially, effective convexity are very sensitive to rounding because they are ratios of very small numbers, so additional precision is needed. The original fair value for this 5-year, 3.50% corporate bond is reported to be 97.0612 in Exhibit II-5. More precisely, the value is 97.06117889

(MV_0). In Exhibit II-12, the fair value for greater precision is 96.83901004 (MV_+) when the par curve is bumped upward. In Exhibit II-13, the fair value is 97.28397531 ($MV-$) when the curve is shifted downward.

The effective duration for this corporate bond is 4.5844 and the effective convexity is 25.8641.

$$\text{Effective Duration} = \frac{97.28397531 - 96.83901004}{2 * 0.0005 * 97.06117889} = 4.5844$$

Effective Convexity

$$= \frac{97.28397531 + 96.83901004 - (2 * 97.06117889)}{(0.0005)^2 * 97.06117889} = 25.8641$$

These statistics can be used to estimate the impact on the corporate bond price following a 50-basis point rise in the benchmark bond yield curve. Similar to equation (10), the estimated change is a drop of 2.1629%.

$$\%\Delta\text{Price} \approx -4.5844 * 0.0050 + \left[1/2 * 25.8641 * (0.0050)^2\right]$$

$$= -0.021629$$

In this example, the differences between the yield and curve durations and convexities are not large (4.4408 vs. 4.5844 and 25.2097 vs. 25.8641). The differences become greater with more shape to the benchmark bond yield curve, a longer time to maturity, and a lower coupon rate. For example, Smith (2014) shows that in 2014 during a time of steep yield curve, a long-term, zero-coupon Treasury bond had a modified duration of 27.635 and an effective duration of 31.415, and a yield convexity of 777.3 and an effective convexity of 940.6.

II.5: Study Questions

Consider a 5-year, 3.25% annual payment, fixed-rate corporate bond assuming a conditional default probability of 1.50% and a recovery rate of 40% for each year.

(A) Calculate the VND, the CVA, the fair value, the yield to maturity and the spread over the 5-year benchmark bond assuming

20% volatility and the original benchmark yield curve. Use the binomial tree in Exhibit I-1. Show the fair value for 8 digits of precision for use in part (C).

(B) Calculate the VND, the CVA, and the fair value assuming 10% volatility, using the binomial tree in Exhibit II-6.

(C) Calculate the effective curve duration and convexity of the corporate bond using a 5-basis point change in the benchmark yield curve. Use the binomial trees in Exhibits II-9 and II-11. Use 8 digits of precision in the fair values.

(D) Use the effective duration and convexity statistics to estimate the change in fair value of the corporate bond following a 100-basis point increase in benchmark bond yields.

II.6: Answers to the Study Questions

(A) The binomial tree and the credit risk table are shown in Exhibit II-14. The VND is 101.1586 (per 100 in par value), the CVA (and DVA) is 4.1488 and the fair value for the 3.25%, 5-year corporate bond is 97.0098. For 8 digits of precision for use in (C), MV_0 is 97.00983862. The yield to maturity is 3.9202% so that the spread is 92.02 basis points given that the yield on the 5-year benchmark bond is 3.00%.

(B) For 10% volatility, the VND is 101.1586, the CVA is 4.1492, and the fair value is 97.0094, as displayed in Exhibit II-15. This confirms the result that the value of a default-free government bond is independent of volatility — it is 101.1586 for both 10% and 20% volatilities. The change in volatility does have a small impact on the fair value because the CVA changes a bit along with the expected loss given default. Higher volatility lowers the credit risk and raises the fair value. The intuition is that when benchmark rates are higher, the bond value falls, so there is less loss if default were to occur. Lower volatility restrains the increase in rates at the top of the tree. That keeps the bond value higher and raises the exposure to loss due to default by the bond issuer.

Exhibit II-14: Valuation of the 3.25%, 5-Year, Annual Coupon Payment Corporate Bond for 20% Volatility

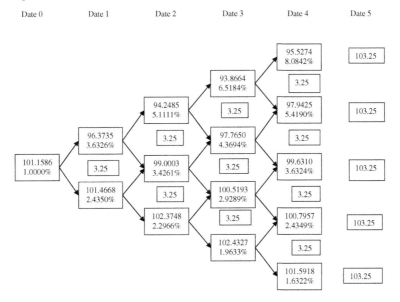

Credit Risk Parameters: 1.50% Conditional Probability of Default, 40% Recovery Rate

Date	Expected Exposure	LGD	POD	Discount Factor	CVA
1	102.1702	61.3021	1.50000%	0.990099	0.9104
2	101.9060	61.1436	1.47750%	0.960978	0.8681
3	102.1440	61.2864	1.46634%	0.928023	0.8277
4	102.6161	61.5697	1.43351%	0.894344	0.7894
5	103.2500	61.9500	1.41200%	0.860968	0.7531
			7.27835%		4.1488

Fair Value = 101.1586 − 4.1488 = 97.0098   (97.00983862)

(C) Exhibits II-16 and II-17 show the binomial trees and credit risk tables for the 5-basis point "bumps" in the benchmark yield curve. The initial and new fair values are: $MV_0 = 97.00983862$, $MV_+ = 96.78671192$, $MV_- = 97.23359647$. The effective duration for the 3.25%, 5-year bond is 4.6066, calculated using equation (11).

$$\text{Effective Duration} = \frac{97.23359647 - 96.78671192}{2 * 0.0005 * 97.00983862} = 4.6066$$

Exhibit II-15: Valuation of the 3.25%, 5-Year, Annual Coupon Payment Corporate Bond Using 10% Volatility

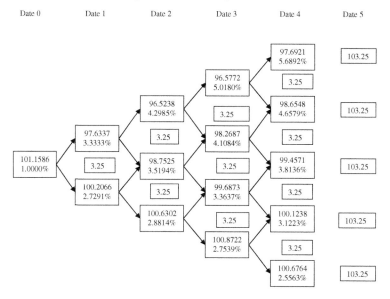

Credit Risk Parameters: 1.50% Conditional Probability of Default, 40% Recovery Rate

Date	Expected Exposure	LGD	POD	Discount Factor	CVA
1	102.1702	61.3021	1.50000%	0.990099	0.9104
2	101.9147	61.1488	1.47750%	0.960978	0.8682
3	102.1647	61.2988	1.46634%	0.928023	0.8279
4	102.6391	61.5835	1.43351%	0.894344	0.7895
5	103.2500	61.9500	1.41200%	0.860968	0.7531
			7.27835%		4.1492

Fair Value = 101.1586 − 4.1492 = 97.0094

From equation (12) the effective convexity is 26.0262.[6]

Effective Convexity

$$= \frac{97.23359647 + 96.78671192 - (2 * 97.00983862)}{(0.0005)^2 * 97.00983862}$$

$$= 26.0262$$

Exhibit II-16: Valuation of 3.25%, 5-Year, Corporate Bond After a 5-Basis-Point Upward Shift in the Benchmark Par Curve

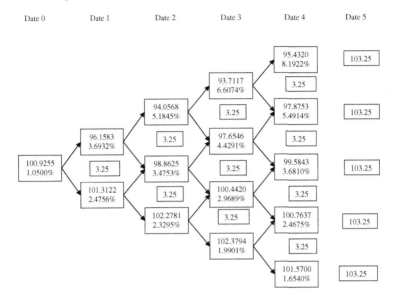

Credit Risk Parameters: 1.50% Conditional Probability of Default, 40% Recovery Rate

Date	Expected Exposure	LGD	POD	Discount Factor	CVA
1	101.9853	61.1912	1.50000%	0.989609	0.9083
2	101.7650	61.0590	1.47750%	0.960032	0.8661
3	102.0476	61.2286	1.46634%	0.926654	0.8257
4	102.5665	61.5399	1.43351%	0.892587	0.7874
5	103.2500	61.9500	1.41200%	0.858854	0.7513
			7.27835%		4.1388

Fair Value = 100.9255 − 4.1388 = 96.7867   (96.78671192)

(D) Given an effective duration of 4.6066 and an effective convexity of 26.0262, the estimated drop in the fair value of the corporate bond is 4.4765%.

$$\%\Delta\text{Price} \approx -4.6066 * 0.0100 + [1/2 * 26.0262 * (0.0100)^2]$$
$$= -0.044765$$

Exhibit II-17: Valuation of the 3.25%, 5-Year, Corporate Bond After a 5-Basis-Point Downward Shift in the Benchmark Par Curve

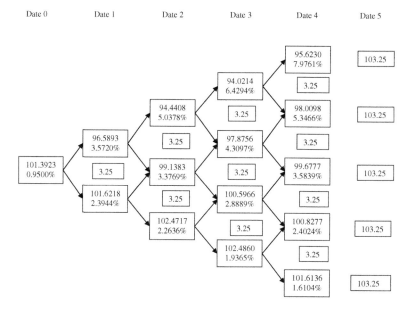

Credit Risk Parameters: 1.50% Conditional Probability of Default, 40% Recovery Rate

Date	Expected Exposure	LGD	POD	Discount Factor	CVA
1	102.3556	61.4133	1.50000%	0.990589	0.9125
2	102.0473	61.2284	1.47750%	0.961926	0.8702
3	102.2405	61.3443	1.46634%	0.929393	0.8297
4	102.6658	61.5995	1.43351%	0.896105	0.7913
5	103.2500	61.9500	1.41200%	0.863088	0.7550
			7.27835%		4.1587

Fair Value = 101.3923 − 4.1587 = 97.2336 (97.23359647)

Endnotes

1. This expression for CVA is based on chapter 7 of Gregory (2010).
2. This numerical example is based on a similar one in Duffie and Singleton (2003).
3. This is based on a general formula for Macaulay duration derived in Smith (2014). Modified duration is the Macaulay duration divided by one plus the yield to maturity per period.
4. This can be obtained using the Excel financial function for modified duration and selecting arbitrary settlement and maturity dates five

years apart:

$$\text{MDURATION}(\text{Date}(2017,10,19),$$
$$\text{Date}(2022,10,19), 0.0350, 0.041632, 1, 0)$$

The inputs are the settlement date, the maturity date, the annual coupon rate, the annual yield to maturity, the periodicity (the payment frequency), and code for the day-count convention. For a bond priced on a coupon payment date, the same result is obtained for a 30/360 day-count (code 0) as for actual/actual (code 1).

5. This is derived in Smith (2014), which also presents closed-form formulas for duration and convexity of a bond between coupon payment dates.

6. 26.0262 is the result of after carrying out the arithmetic shown. Because the calculation is very sensitive to rounding, the result is 26.0240 when done on a spreadsheet and linking in the numbers.

Chapter III

Valuing Floating-Rate Notes
and Interest Rate Caps and Floors

Floating-rate notes (called FRNs or just "floaters") were introduced in the 1970s to offer bond investors protection from higher market interest rates resulting from higher inflation, which reached double digits levels in those years. On a traditional fixed-rate bond, rate volatility is manifest entirely in the price of the security because its scheduled interest payments are fixed. Naturally, higher market rates lead to falling bond market values. A floater, on the other hand, transfers that interest rate volatility to future cash flows, thereby minimizing current price fluctuations and preserving capital value for investors. Of course, an FRN is still subject to price movements arising from changes in credit risk.

A corporation might choose to issue a floating-rate note for several reasons. One is that financing at the short-term end of the yield curve historically has offered a lower cost of funds than longer-maturity debt because the government bond benchmark yield curve typically is upwardly sloped. In addition, credit spreads are also increasing with the time to maturity. Another reason is that some corporations have net operating revenues that are positively correlated with the business cycle (for instance, luxury goods manufacturers or freight companies). Countercyclical monetary policy generally leads to positive correlation between interest rates and the business cycle. Therefore, floating-rate debt provides a natural "internal" hedge of interest rate risk for these firms — interest expense is lower (higher) when revenues are lower (higher). A third motivation occurs with corporations having substantial amounts of cash holdings that are invested in the money market. Financing these cash assets with floating-rate debt minimizes risk and avoids the "negative carry" if fixed-rate debt is issued and the yield curve remains upwardly sloped.[1]

The 1980s were a time of substantial financial market innovation, driven by technological developments that allowed for management of complex cash flows (for example, mortgage-backed securities) and also by demand for securities that allowed institutional investors and corporate issuers alike to "express a view" on the future path for interest rates. Interest rate volatility was at an historical high, in part because of monetary policy (the "Volcker experiment" with targeting the growth rate of the money supply instead of the fed funds rate). *Structured notes* became popular; often these were FRNs that were embellished with embedded derivatives. Before illustrating the impact of the embedded option on the value of a capped FRN, it is appropriate to start with a traditional (or "straight") floater.

III.1: CVA and Discount Margin on a Straight Floater

Exhibit III-1 illustrates how the binomial forward rate tree model can be used to calculate the value of a 5-year, floating-rate corporate bond that pays annually the 1-year benchmark rate plus 1.00%. This is the hallmark of a straight floater — the interest payment for each time period is based on a money market reference rate plus a fixed spread. This is different than a step-up or step-down fixed-rate note in which the coupon interest payment varies period to period by a preset amount specified at issuance in the documentation. The coupon interest rate on a floater varies according to observed changes in market rates as time passes. Directly across from each node in the tree in Exhibit III-1 is the realized interest payment. Note that floaters typically pay interest *in arrears*, meaning that the observation for the reference rate is determined at the beginning of the

Exhibit III-1: Valuation of a 5-Year, Floating-Rate Corporate Bond Paying the 1-Year Rate + 1.00%

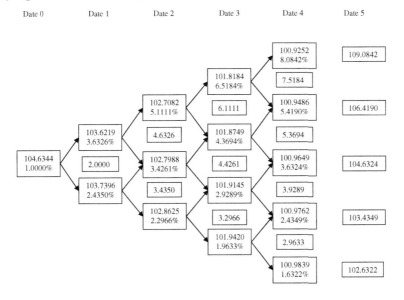

Credit Risk Parameters:
    1.50% Conditional Probability of Default, 40% Recovery Rate for Dates 1, 2, 3
    3.00% Conditional Probability of Default, 20% Recovery Rate for Dates 4, 5

Date	Expected Exposure	LGD	POD	Discount Factor	CVA
1	105.6808	63.4085	1.50000%	0.990099	0.9417
2	106.8259	64.0955	1.47750%	0.960978	0.9101
3	106.4560	63.8736	1.45534%	0.928023	0.8627
4	105.7595	84.6076	2.86701%	0.894344	2.1694
5	104.9329	83.9463	2.78100%	0.860968	2.0100
			10.08086%		6.8938

Fair Value = 104.6344 – 6.8938 = 97.7406 (97.74058355)

period and the interest payment is made to the investor at the end of the period.

On Date 2, the interest payment to the investor is 4.6326 per 100 of par value when the 1-year rate is 3.6326% on Date 1. The fixed spread of 1.00%, which is called the *quoted margin*, is added to the reference rate to get the interest payment. At maturity on Date 5, the total payment is 102.6322 when the reference rate is 1.6322% on Date 4. In practice, the interest rate on floaters typically is reset and paid monthly, quarterly, or semiannually. Then, an additional term needed to get the interest payment is the *day-count factor* for the time period (e.g., actual/360 or actual/365). Here, with annual payments for simplicity, that factor drops out as each year is assumed to have 360 or 365 days.

The VND for this corporate floater is 104.6344, calculated in Exhibit III-1 via backward induction through the binomial tree. Another approach to get the value assuming no default is to recognize that this straight floating-rate note paying the 1-year rate plus 1.00% can be interpreted as a combination of a floater paying the 1-year rate *flat*, meaning no margin over the reference rate, and a 5-year annuity paying 1.00% of the principal amount each year. The VND for a floater paying the 1-year rate flat would be 100.0000 — each interest payment at the end of the year matches the 1-year rate observed at the beginning of the year for all nodes in the tree. The floater would always be worth par value on an interest rate reset date, independent of rate volatility. The present value of the annuity paying 1.00% of principal each year is 4.6344 (per 100 of par value), calculated using the discount factors from Exhibit I-3.

$$(1.0 * 0.990099) + (1.0 * 0.960978) + (1.0 * 0.928023)$$
$$+ (1.0 * 0.894344) + (1.0 * 0.860968) = 4.6344$$

Therefore, the VND for the FRN paying the 1-year rate plus 1.00% is 104.6344(= 100 + 4.6344).

The credit risk on this floater is calculated in the lower portion of Exhibit III-1. The expected exposure to default loss for each date is the sum of two probability-weighted averages, one for the expected value of the FRN and the other for the expected interest payment. For each, the probabilities are taken from the binomial forward rate tree in Exhibit I-1. For example, the expected exposure for Date 4 is 105.7595.

$$[(0.0625 * 100.9252) + (0.2500 * 100.9486) + (0.3750 * 100.9649)$$
$$+ (0.2500 * 100.9762) + (0.0625 * 100.9839)]$$
$$+ [(0.1250 * 7.5184) + (0.3750 * 5.3694) + (0.3750 * 3.9289)$$
$$+ (0.1250 * 2.9633)] = 100.9624 + 4.7971 = 105.7595$$

The expected value of the FRN on Date 4 is 100.9624, the first term in brackets, calculated using the Date-4 probabilities of arriving at the nodes in the tree. The expected interest payment is 4.7971, which is based on the Date-3 probabilities because interest is paid in arrears.

To illustrate the versatility of the tabular methodology to allow for a term structure of credit risk, the conditional probability of default is assumed to be 1.50% per year for the first three years and then to go up to 3.00% for the fourth and fifth years. Similarly, the recovery rate is assumed to be 40% for Dates 1, 2, and 3, and then to go down to 20% for the last two years. The loss severities are 60% and 80%, respectively. Presumably, there is a significant change in the projected credit risk of the bond issuer after the third year. This could reflect an anticipated change in the legal, regulatory, or competitive environment facing the issuer, for instance, the end of patent protection on a key product or a disruptive technological advance expected to be available to competitors in a few years.

The probabilities of default and survival for Date 1 are 1.50% and 98.50%, respectively. For Date 2, they are 1.47750% (=1.50% * 98.50%) and 97.02250% (=98.50% − 1.47750%). For Date 3, they are 1.45534% (=1.50% * 97.02250%) and 95.56716% (=97.02250% − 1.45534%). The conditional probability of default doubles for Date 4 so that the probability of default (POD) is 2.86701% (=3.00% * 95.56716%) and survival probability is 92.70015% (=95.56716% − 2.86701%). The POD for Date 5 is 2.78100% (=3.00% * 92.70015%). Overall, the probability that the investor experiences no default by the maturity on Date 5 is 89.91914% (=92.70015% − 2.78100%) and the cumulative probability of default is 10.08086% (the sum of the PODs).

The fair value for the floating-rate corporate note is 97.7406, the difference between the VND of 104.6344 and the CVA of 6.8938. Floaters usually are issued at, or very close to, par value. This FRN has fallen to a discount below par value because of the heightened credit risk (or, perhaps a change in liquidity or taxation). Said differently, the quoted margin of 1.00% is not sufficient for the note to trade at par value on an interest rate reset date. A statistic used by investors to compare floaters is the *discount margin*, the fixed spread over the reference rate that reflects the current extent of credit risk on the floater.

There are two ways to calculate the discount margin. The first method is to solve by trial-and-error search (or use a search routine like GoalSeek or Solver in Excel) for the margin over the 1-year benchmark rates in the binomial tree such that the fair value rounds to 100.0000. This is displayed in Exhibit III-2. It turns out that the discount margin is 1.50461%. At that spread over the 1-year rate, all the interest payments and values in the tree are higher than in

Exhibit III-2: First Method to Calculate the Discount Margin on the 5-Year, Floating-Rate Corporate Bond Paying the 1-Year Rate +1.00%

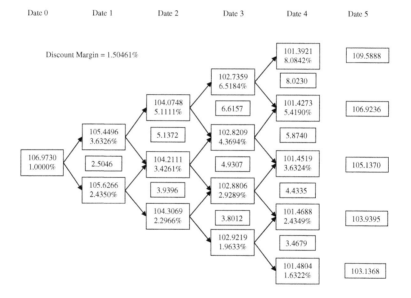

Credit Risk Parameters:
    1.50% Conditional Probability of Default, 40% Recovery Rate for Dates 1, 2, 3
    3.00% Conditional Probability of Default, 20% Recovery Rate for Dates 4, 5

Date	Expected Exposure	LGD	POD	Discount Factor	CVA
1	108.0427	64.8256	1.50000%	0.990099	0.9628
2	108.7394	65.2436	1.47750%	0.960978	0.9264
3	107.9149	64.7489	1.45534%	0.928023	0.8745
4	106.7497	85.3998	2.86701%	0.894344	2.1897
5	105.4375	84.3500	2.78100%	0.860968	2.0196
			10.08086%		6.9730

Fair Value = 106.9730 – 6.9730 = 100.0000

Exhibit III-1. For instance, the interest payment on Date 1 is 2.5046 per 100 of par value, the initial 1-year rate of 1.00% plus the discount margin of 1.50461%, times 100 (and rounded to four decimals). The VND would be 106.9730, the CVA 6.9730, and the value on Date 0 is 100.0000.

The second method is to leave the quoted margin intact at 1.00% and to solve for the spread over the 1-year benchmark rates such that when the interest payments and bond values are discounted at that rate, the present value equals 97.7406, which is the fair value of the FRN. This is carried out by trial-and-error search. This is shown in Exhibit III-3. Here, the discount margin turns out to be 1.50874%. On Date 2 if the benchmark rate is 5.1111%, the bond value is 98.6601:

$$\frac{6.1111 + (0.50 * 99.0940 + 0.50 * 99.0663)]}{1 + 0.051111 + 0.0150874} = 98.6601$$

Exhibit III-3: Second Method to Calculate the Discount Margin on the 5-Year,Floating-Rate Corporate Bond Paying the 1-Year Rate +1.00%

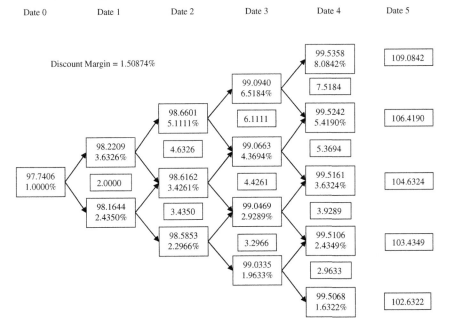

On Date 0, the bond value is 97.7406:

$$\frac{2.0000 + (0.50 * 98.2209 + 0.50 * 98.1644)]}{1 + 0.010000 + 0.0150874} = 97.7406$$

Notice that the same discount margin is used in addition to the 1-year benchmark rate to discount each of the expected future values and interest payment.

In the first method the credit risk is embodied in the CVA calculation; in the second it is in the spread over the benchmark rate. That the results are virtually the same, 1.50461% and 1.50874% (the small difference is due to rounding), reinforces the idea that the CVA and the credit spread each represent the credit risk on the bond. In general, a floating-rate note is priced at a discount to par value when the discount margin is greater than the quoted margin. It is priced at a premium when the discount margin is less than the quoted margin.

III.2: A Capped Floating-Rate Note

A *capped* floating-rate note places a ceiling on the interest rate paid to the investor. Exhibit III-4 shows the valuation of a 5-year, floating-rate corporate note that annually pays the 1-year benchmark rate plus a quoted margin of 1.00%, subject to a maximum of 6.00%. The credit risk of the corporate issuer is assumed to be the same as with the straight floater in the previous example that did not contain an embedded option. Given that assumption, the difference between the values of the straight floater and the capped floater is the implied value of the embedded derivative. The assumed conditional probability of default for the capped floating-rate note is still 1.50% for three years and then 3.00% for the final two years. The assumed loss severity rises from 60% to 80% after the third year.

Notice in Exhibit III-4 that the 6% maximum refers to the interest rate including the quoted margin. Therefore, the rate ceiling becomes binding at the nodes in the tree where the 1-year benchmark rates exceed 5.00%. This is projected to occur first on Date 2 if the 1-year rate is 5.1111%. Then the Date-3 interest payment is constrained to be 6 per 100 of par value. On Date 3 the embedded

Exhibit III-4: Valuation of a 5-Year, Capped Floating-Rate Corporate Bond Paying the 1-Year Rate + 1.00%, Subject to a Maximum of 6.00%

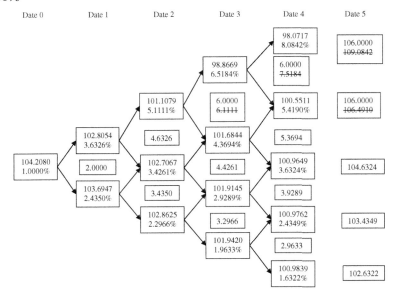

Credit Risk Parameters:
    1.50% Conditional Probability of Default, 40% Recovery Rate for Dates 1, 2, 3
    3.00% Conditional Probability of Default, 20% Recovery Rate for Dates 4, 5

Date	Expected Exposure	LGD	POD	Discount Factor	CVA
1	105.2500	63.1500	1.50000%	0.990099	0.9379
2	106.3798	63.8279	1.47750%	0.960978	0.9063
3	105.9879	63.5927	1.45534%	0.928023	0.8589
4	105.2919	84.2336	2.86701%	0.894344	2.1598
5	104.6354	83.7083	2.78100%	0.860968	2.0043
			10.08086%		6.8671

Fair Value = 104.2080 – 6.8671 = 97.3409

option is binding at the top of the tree where the 1-year rate is 6.5184% and on Date 4 if the rate is 5.4190% or 8.0842%. Working through the tree via backward induction produces a VND for the capped floater of 104.2080, the value assuming no default. The CVA is 6.8671 given the assumed parameters for credit risk and the fair value of the bond is 97.3409.

The value of the embedded option — a 5-year, 5% interest rate cap on the 1-year benchmark rate — can be inferred from the results from Exhibit III-1 for the straight floater and Exhibit III-4 for the capped floater.

	VND	CVA	Fair Value
Straight FRN	104.6344	6.8938	97.7406
Capped FRN	104.2080	6.8671	97.3409
Embedded Option	0.4264	0.0267	0.3997

The value of the embedded interest rate cap is 42.64 basis points neglecting default risk. However, the value is 39.97 basis points once credit risk is factored into the valuation model. The small difference, 2.67 basis points, arises because the expected exposure to default loss for each date is slightly lower on the capped floater. The ceiling on the interest payment reduces the potential loss if the issuer defaults. To discuss the decision by the corporation to issue the capped floater, it is instructive to consider a standalone interest rate cap and the strategy of issuing the straight floater and separately buying protection from higher interest rates.

III.3: A Standalone Interest Rate Cap

Interest rate *cap and floor agreements* are multi-period *options* on a reference rate. An interest rate cap benefits the holder in time periods when the reference rate is *above* the designated cap strike rate. A rate floor pays the holder when the reference rate is *below* the floor rate. The amount of the settlement payment, which typically is paid in arrears as on a floating-rate note, is the rate difference times the *notional principal*, times the day-count factor. The principal is "notional" because that amount is not exchanged between the counterparties; it merely is the scale factor for determining the size of the transaction and the settlement payments.

An *interest rate cap* can be interpreted as a series of *put options* on a hypothetical, 1-period, par value, benchmark bond that pays the specified cap rate. For example, suppose that the cap rate is 5% and the notional principal is 100 for annual settlement in arrears.

The option holder has the right, but not the obligation, to *sell* to the option writer for a price of 100 a 1-year benchmark bond that pays 105 at the end of the year. If the 1-year rate is above 5% in one of the time periods, say 6.5184%, the put option is exercised because the value of the bond is below 100 — in fact, bond price would be 98.5745 (= 105/1.065184). As expected, the put option gains when the price falls (and the rate rises).

Similarly, an *interest rate floor* can be viewed as a series of *call options* on a hypothetical 1-period benchmark bond that pays the preset floor rate. The holder would exercise the option to *buy* the 5% bond for 100 if the 1-year reference rate is below 5%, say 4.3694%. The bond price would be 100.6042 (= 105/1.043694). The call option gains when the price rises (and the rate falls).

Interest rate caps and floors are strictly *cash-settled* derivatives — the option cannot be settled by physical delivery of the 1-period bond. Moreover, a 5%, 1-year benchmark bond might not even exist. If the reference rate is 6.5184%, the cap writer simply pays the holder 1.5184 per 100 of notional principal at the end of the year: (6.5184% − 5%) ∗ 100 = 1.5184. [In general, this also is multiplied by the day-count factor, for instance, if settlements are quarterly or semiannually]. If the reference rate is equal to or less than the 5% strike rate, the cap writer pays nothing — the option is "out of the money". If the reference rate is 4.3694%, the floor writer pays the holder 0.6306 per 100 of the notional amount: (5% − 4.3694%) ∗ 100 = 0.6306 and zero if the reference rate exceeds the strike rate.

While in principle an interest rate cap is a series of put options on a 1-period bond and a floor is a series of call options — and when the market first developed in the 1980s they were documented as such — derivative traders in practice refer to them differently. Most interest rate caps and floors in the U.S. market are based on LIBOR, in particular, on 3-month LIBOR. An interest rate cap agreement to a trader becomes a "call on LIBOR" and a floor a "put on LIBOR". This terminology follows from the payoff diagrams on a settlement date for buying and writing a cap and a floor, which are shown in Exhibit III-5 for a 5% strike rate. In the language of over-the-counter derivatives,

Exhibit III-5: Payoff Diagrams for an Interest Rate Cap and an Interest Rate Floor

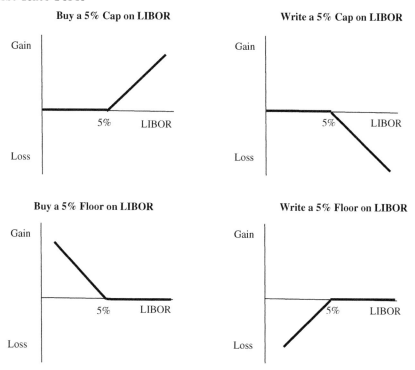

the commodity being trading is the reference rate, 3-month LIBOR. A rate cap conveys to the holder the right to "buy LIBOR" at the cap rate and a rate floor the right to "sell LIBOR" at the floor rate.

A salient feature of interest rate cap and floor agreements is unilateral credit risk (unlike interest rate swaps that have bilateral credit risk). The cap or floor contract once purchased is always an asset to its holder and a liability to its writer. Typically, the premium for the multi-period option contract is paid up-front and is quoted in basis points. If the cap premium is 185 basis points and the notional principal $100 million, the price is $1.85 million. After that initial exchange, the derivative has a non-negative value to the buyer. That amount is the value assuming no default (VND) less the credit valuation adjustment (CVA) that reflects the assumed probability of default by the cap or floor writer and the recovery rate. This calculation is

Exhibit III-6: Valuation of a 5-Year, 5% Interest Rate Cap on the 1-Year Rate

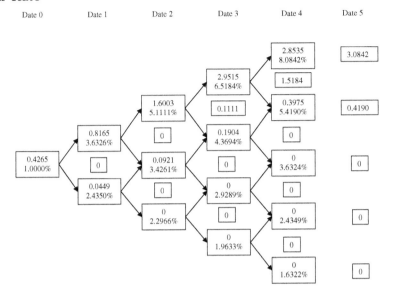

Credit Risk Parameters: 0.50% Conditional Probability of Default, 10% Recovery Rate

Date	Expected Exposure	LGD	POD	Discount Factor	CVA
1	0.4307	0.3876	0.50000%	0.990099	0.0019
2	0.4461	0.4015	0.49750%	0.960978	0.0019
3	0.4681	0.4213	0.49501%	0.928023	0.0019
4	0.4675	0.4208	0.49254%	0.894344	0.0019
5	0.2975	0.2678	0.49007%	0.860968	0.0011
			2.47512%		0.0088

Fair Value = 0.4265 − 0.0088 = 0.4177

displayed in Exhibit III-6 for a 5-year, non-collateralized standalone interest rate cap that references the 1-year rate on a benchmark bond and has a strike rate of 5%. If the cap is not collateralized, counterparty credit risk is a concern to the buyer of the contract. Issues regarding collateralization are covered in Chapters V and VI on interest rate swaps.

The VND for this interest rate cap agreement is 0.4265 per 100 notional principal, or 42.65 basis points. For a notional principal of $100 million, the value assuming no default is $426,500. The cap delivers payments to the holder at the top of the tree at the nodes where the 1-year benchmark rate exceeds the 5% cap strike rate. If the rate on Date 4 is 5.4190%, the payment on Date 5 at the end of year is 0.4190 per 100 of notional principal: $(0.054190 - 0.0500) * 100 = 0.4190$. On Date 2 when the 1-year rate is 5.1111%, the cap value is 1.6003:

$$\frac{[(0.051111 - 0.0500) * 100] + [(0.50 * 2.9515 + 0.50 * 0.1904)]}{1.051111}$$
$$= 1.6003$$

The first term in the numerator is the settlement payment on Date 3 and the second term is the expected value of the cap on Date 3. The Date-0 value is 0.4265 — this is the same as the difference between the VND for the straight floater in Exhibit III-1 and the VND for the capped floater in Exhibit III-4 (when those values are not rounded to four decimals).

The assumptions for the credit risk posed by the cap writer are shown in Exhibit III-6 below the tree. The assumed conditional probability of default for each year is 0.50%. The assumed recovery rate is just 10%, so the loss severity is 90%. The cap writer here presumably is a money center commercial bank. As a highly regulated financial institution, the probability of default is deemed to be low.[2] However, if default occurs, the recovery rate is assumed to be rather low because depositors stand ahead of unsecured creditors in the priority of claim. The CVA is 0.0088, so the fair value inclusive of credit risk is 0.4177.

Some issuers of floating-rate debt prefer to address the risk of higher short-term rates by acquiring rate protection in the form of an interest rate cap on a money market reference rate. In practice, this is usually on 3-month LIBOR. This can be accomplished by issuing the straight floater and buying a *standalone* interest rate cap or by issuing a capped floater that contains an *embedded* rate cap. In the examples here, the small difference (39.97 basis points for the value of the embedded derivative and 41.77 basis points for the standalone cap) arises from the source of the credit risk. When the cap is embedded in the debt liability, the credit risk of the issuer of the capped floater matters whereas it is the default probability and loss severity associated with the writer of the cap agreement that determines the fair value when the derivative is a separate contract.

A motive for issuing a structured note can be differential pricing of embedded versus standalone derivatives. Some corporate issuers over the years have found that a lower cost of borrowed funds can be obtained by issuing a security containing embedded derivatives and then reversing those exposures with standalone contracts. While this likely entails a more innovative offering such as an inverse or a bear floater (which are discussed in Chapter VII on structured notes), the capped floating-rate note serves as an example. The corporation issues the FRN paying the 1-year benchmark rate plus 1.00% subject to a maximum of 6.00% and writes a comparable standalone cap.

This can be described using the "arithmetic of financial engineering" as follows[3]:

$$-\text{Capped FRN} = -\text{Straight FRN} + \text{Interest Rate Cap} \qquad (1)$$

The "−" sign indicates a liability and the "+" sign an asset. In equation (1), the issuer of the capped FRN is implicitly "long" the rate cap. Writing a standalone interest rate cap can neutralize this long position. That cap is then sold back to the bank that underwrites the debt offering. Re-arranging equation (1) shows that a straight floating-rate debt liability is created by issuing the capped FRN and going "short" a standalone rate cap:

$$-\text{Straight FRN} = -\text{Capped FRN} - \text{Interest Rate Cap} \qquad (2)$$

Note that if the corporation chooses this strategy, the premium received on selling the cap would be 39.97 basis points — the fair value that reflects the credit risk of the corporation.

III.4: Effective Duration and Convexity of a Floating-Rate Note

The effective duration and convexity statistics for a floater can be calculated using the binomial trees. The 5-year, corporate straight floater paying the 1-year rate plus 1.00% examined in Section III.1

has a fair value of 97.7406. Exhibit III-1 shows that the VND is 104.6344 and the CVA is 6.8938 based on a conditional default probability that is expected to rise from 1.50% to 3.00% after the third year and a recovery rate that falls from 40% to 20%.

A decision needs to be made about the assumed timing of the shifts to the benchmark bond par curve on Date 0 to calculate the effective duration and convexity of a floating-rate note (and interest rate derivatives such as swaps, caps, and floors). Exhibits II-8 and II-10 in Chapter II implicitly assume that the shifts occur *before* the rate is set for the interest payment due on Date 1. If the par curve shifts upward, the payment is 2.05 per 100 of par value (the 1-year rate of 1.05% plus the 1.00% quoted margin); if the curve shifts downward, the payment is 1.95 (the 1-year rate of 0.95% plus 1.00%). An alternative assumption is that the 1-year rate is set at 1.00% for Date 0 and the shifts only affect subsequent rate settings — that would have a significant impact on the risk statistics.

Exhibit III-7 shows results using eight digits of precision in reporting the fair values. The trees for the bumped curves and the CVA calculations are not exhibited. The effective duration of the

Exhibit III-7: Effective Duration and Convexity of a Floating-Rate Note 5-Year, Floating-Rate Corporate Bond Paying the 1-Year Rate +1.00%

	Fair Value
MV_0 (Exhibit III-1)	97.74058355
MV_+	97.74246571
MV_-	97.73869766

Credit Risk Parameters: 1.50% to 3.00% Default Probability, 40% to 20% Recovery Rate

$$\text{Effective Duration} = \frac{97.73869766 - 97.74246571}{2 * 0.0005 * 97.74058355} = -0.0386$$

$$\text{Effective Convexity} = \frac{97.73869766 + 97.74246571 - (2 * 97.74058355)}{(0.0005)^2 * 97.74058355} = -0.1514$$

FRN is −0.0386, and the effective convexity is −0.1514. That these numbers are small is to be expected given the assumption that any change in benchmark rates on Date 0 impacts the next payment — the floater's price sensitivity should be close to zero. It is perhaps surprising that they are negative, albeit slightly negative. When the benchmark bond par curve shifts upward, the fair value of the floater goes up slightly — from 97.7406 to 97.7425. A positive relationship between market interest rates and the value of a debt security is rare on traditional debt securities.

The duration of the floating-rate note is negative because the debt security is trading at a discount below par value. Exhibits III-2 and III-3 demonstrate that the discount margin for the floating-rate note is on the order of 1.50%. Because investors receive only 1.00% over the 1-year rate, the amount of the discount below par reflects the present value of the "deficiency" in the projected interest payments. If there is no change in the credit risk of the issuer when benchmark rates are bumped upward, as is assumed here, the present value of that deficiency (that is, the annuity for the difference between the discount margin and the quoted margin) goes down. That reduces the amount of the discount and raises the price slightly. When the par curve is shifted downward, the present value of the deficiency goes up. That increases the discount and the price goes down a bit. Therefore, the effective duration is negative. If the floating-rate note has a fair value at a premium above par value, its effective duration (and convexity) is slightly positive.[4]

III.5: The Impact of Volatility on the Capped Floater

As with the traditional fixed-rate bond having no embedded options, there will be a minor impact on the value of a straight floater following a change in the assumed volatility of forward rates. This is due to the small change in the expected exposure to default loss. Naturally, there will be a greater effect when the floating-rate note contains an option that is directly influenced by the range of interest rates

Exhibit III-8: Valuation of a 5-Year, Capped Floating-Rate Corporate Bond Paying the 1-Year Rate + 1.00%, Subject to a Maximum of 6.00%, for 10% Volatility

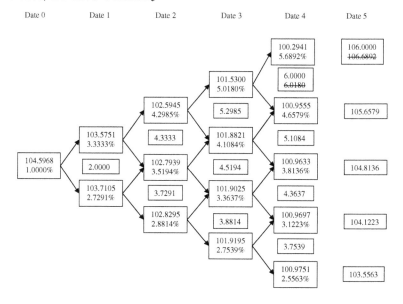

Credit Risk Parameters:
    1.50% Conditional Probability of Default, 40% Recovery Rate for Dates 1, 2, 3
    3.00% Conditional Probability of Default, 20% Recovery Rate for Dates 4, 5

Date	Expected Exposure	LGD	POD	Discount Factor	CVA
1	105.6428	63.3857	1.50000%	0.990099	0.9414
2	106.7842	64.0705	1.47750%	0.960978	0.9097
3	106.4051	63.8430	1.45534%	0.928023	0.8623
4	105.6931	84.5545	2.86701%	0.894344	2.1681
5	104.8474	83.8779	2.78100%	0.860968	2.0083
			10.08086%		6.8897

Fair Value = 104.5968 − 6.8897 = 97.7071

for future dates. This is illustrated with the embedded rate restriction in the 5-year, *capped* corporate floating-rate note that pays the 1-year benchmark rate plus 1.00% subject to a maximum of 6.00%. Exhibit III-8 shows the valuation using the binomial tree for 10% volatility shown in Exhibit II-6 in Chapter II.

The following table summarizes the impact on the value of the capped floater.

Volatility Assumption	VND	CVA	Fair Value
10%, in Exhibit III-8	104.5968	6.8897	97.7071
20%, in Exhibit III-4	104.2080	6.8671	97.3409
Difference	0.3888	0.0226	0.3662

The assumed default probabilities and recovery rates are the same as the straight floater. When the volatility is lowered to 10%, the increase of 0.3662 in the fair value ($= 97.7071 - 97.3409$) is largely due to the increase by 0.3888 in VND ($= 104.5968 - 104.2080$), offset slightly by the increase of 0.0226 in CVA ($= 6.8897 - 6.8671$).

These results indicate that lower volatility raises the value of the capped floater to the investor. This is explained by rearranging equation (2):

$$+\text{Capped FRN} = +\text{Straight FRN} - \text{Interest Rate Cap} \qquad (3)$$

Buying a capped FRN is equivalent in terms of promised net cash flow (but not equivalent in terms of credit risk) to buying a straight floater having no rate restrictions and *writing* an interest rate cap. Lowering volatility reduces the value of the cap — settlement payments and values are lower because of the narrower range in projected future rates. Because the investor has an implicit short position in the cap, the lower value increases the value of the capped floater. However, the higher values for the capped floater due to the lower volatility assumption also increase the expected exposure to default loss. Therefore, the change in the VND is greater than the change in the fair value when the assumed level of interest rate volatility is changed.

III.6: Study Questions

(A) Consider a 5-year, floating-rate corporate bond that pays the 1-year benchmark rate plus 1.50%. Assume a conditional default probability of 1.25% and a recovery rate of 30% for each year.

Calculate the VND, the CVA, the fair value, the discount margin assuming 20% volatility and the original benchmark yield curve. Use the binomial tree in Exhibit I-1.

(B) Consider a 5-year corporate "floored floater" that pays the 1-year benchmark rate plus 1.50% subject to a minimum of 4.00%. Assume a conditional default probability of 1.25% and a recovery rate of 30% for each year. Calculate the VND, the CVA, and the fair value for the floored floater. Calculate the

Exhibit III-9: Valuation of a 5-Year, Floating-Rate Corporate Bond Paying the 1-Year Rate +1.50%

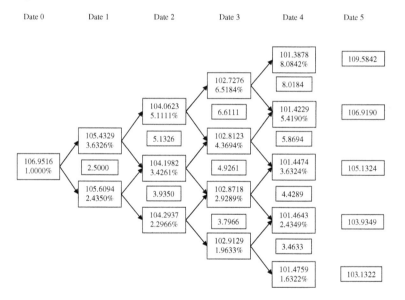

Credit Risk Parameters: 1.25% Conditional Probability of Default, 30% Recovery Rate

Date	Expected Exposure	LGD	POD	Discount Factor	CVA
1	108.0211	75.6148	1.25000%	0.990099	0.9358
2	108.7219	76.1053	1.23438%	0.960978	0.9028
3	107.9016	75.5311	1.21895%	0.928023	0.8544
4	106.7407	74.7185	1.20371%	0.894344	0.8044
5	105.4329	73.8030	1.18866%	0.860968	0.7553
			6.09569%		4.2527

Fair Value = 106.9516 – 4.2527 = 102.6989

value of the embedded interest rate floor having a strike rate of 2.50%. Calculate the value of a standalone 2.50% interest rate floor using the same credit risk parameters.

III.7: Answers to the Study Questions

(A) As shown in Exhibit III-9, the VND for the floater is 106.9516 (per 100 of par value). Notice that the values in the binomial

Exhibit III-10: First Method to Calculate the Discount Margin on the 5-Year, Floating-Rate Corporate Bond Paying the 1-Year Rate +1.50%

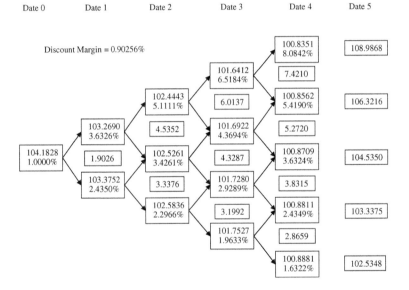

Credit Risk Parameters: 1.25% Conditional Probability of Default, 30% Recovery Rate

Date	Expected Exposure	LGD	POD	Discount Factor	CVA
1	105.2247	73.6573	1.25000%	0.990099	0.9116
2	106.4564	74.5195	1.23438%	0.960978	0.8840
3	106.1743	74.3220	1.21895%	0.928023	0.8407
4	105.5682	73.8978	1.20371%	0.894344	0.7955
5	104.8355	73.3848	1.18866%	0.860968	0.7510
			6.09569%		4.1828

Fair Value = 104.1828 − 4.1828 = 100.0000

tree for each date are very similar. That is the essence of a
floating-rate note — interest rate volatility impacts the interest
payments while the market value remains essentially the same.
For each date, the value is a bit lower as the 1-year benchmark
is higher. For instance, it is 101.4759 on Date 4 at the bottom
of the tree and 101.3878 at the top. That is because the quoted
margin, here 1.50%, is fixed. The CVA is 4.2527 and the fair
value is 102.6989 (= 106.9516 − 4.2527).

The discount margin is 0.90256% using the first method
described in Section III.1 and 0.90254% using the second
method. The first method, shown in Exhibit III-10, uses trial-
and-error search to solve for the margin over the benchmark
rate such that the fair value after subtracting the CVA from
the VND rounds to 100.0000. The floating-rate note is priced
at a premium to par value and the discount margin is less than

**Exhibit III-11: Second Method to Calculate the Discount Margin on
the 5-Year,Floating-Rate Corporate Bond Paying the 1-Year Rate
+1.50%**

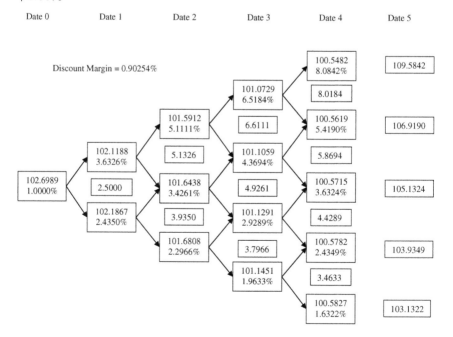

the quoted margin (0.90254% < 1.50%). The credit rating on this FRN likely has been upgraded since issuance. Investors now would be willing to accept a margin of only 90.256 basis points to buy the security at par value.

The second method obtains virtually the same result but using a different approach. As shown in Exhibit III-11, the discount margin is added to the benchmark rate when discounting the expected future value and the scheduled interest payment.

Exhibit III-12: Valuation of a 5-Year, Floored Floating-Rate Corporate Bond Paying the 1-Year Rate +1.50%, Subject to a Minimum of 4.00%

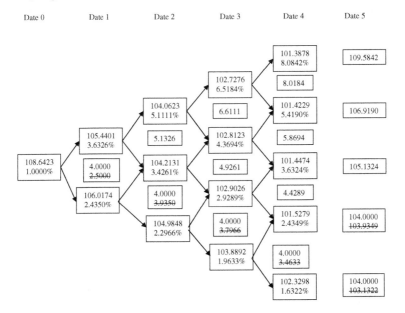

Credit Risk Parameters: 1.25% Conditional Probability of Default, 30% Recovery Rate

Date	Expected Exposure	LGD	POD	Discount Factor	CVA
1	109.7288	76.8101	1.25000%	0.990099	0.9506
2	108.9346	76.2542	1.23438%	0.960978	0.9045
3	108.0860	75.6602	1.21895%	0.928023	0.8559
4	106.8770	74.8139	1.20371%	0.894344	0.8054
5	105.5034	73.8524	1.18866%	0.860968	0.7558
			6.09569%		4.2722

Fair Value = 108.6423 − 4.2722 = 104.3701

Notice that the credit risk table is not needed and would be double-counting the default risk.

(B) The calculations for the floored floater are presented in Exhibit III-12, which parallel those for the capped FRN in Exhibit III-4. In this case the interest payment is the maximum of the benchmark rate plus 1.50% and the floor set at 4.00%. This is a binding constraint on Date 0 and then on the later dates in the lower portion of the binomial tree whenever the benchmark rate is less than 2.50%. The VND is 108.6423, the CVA is 4.2722, and the fair value is 104.3701.

Exhibit III-13: Valuation of a 5-Year, 2.50% Interest Rate Floor on the 1-Year Rate

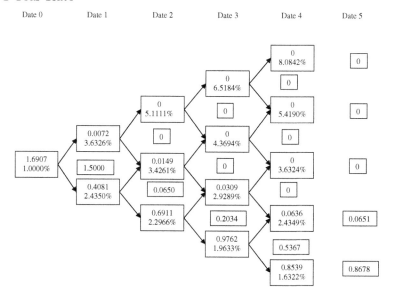

Credit Risk Parameters: 1.25% Conditional Probability of Default, 30% Recovery Rate

Date	Expected Exposure	LGD	POD	Discount Factor	CVA
1	1.7076	1.1953	1.25000%	0.990099	0.0148
2	0.2127	0.1489	1.23438%	0.960978	0.0018
3	0.1845	0.1291	1.21895%	0.928023	0.0015
4	0.1363	0.0954	1.20371%	0.894344	0.0010
5	0.0705	0.0494	1.18866%	0.860968	0.0005
			6.09569%		0.0196

Fair Value = 1.6907 – 0.0196 = 1.6712

The fair value of the straight floater in part (A) is 102.6989, as displayed in Exhibit III-9. The value of the embedded 2.50% interest rate floor is 1.6712 ($= 104.3701 - 102.6989$). The purchase of the floored floater can be interpreted as the purchase of a straight floater and a standalone interest rate floor.

$$+\text{Floored FRN} = +\text{Straight FRN} + \text{Interest Rate Floor} \quad (4)$$

Because these valuations are done under the assumption of no-arbitrage, it is no surprise that the value of the 2.50% standalone interest rate floor is also 1.6712, using the same credit risk parameters. This is demonstrated in Exhibit III-13. The expected exposure and the LGD show that most of the credit risk rests on Date 1.

Endnotes

1. These motivations for issuing floating-rate debt are discussed further in Adams and Smith (2013). That paper argues that some firms benefit by issuing a "synthetic floater", meaning the issuance of a traditional fixed-rate bond combined with a receive-fixed interest rate swap.
2. A default probability of 0.50% is in reality much too high for a major financial institution, which likely has been designated to be "systemically important" by regulators — 0.10% is more realistic. The 0.50% assumption is chosen to simplify calculation and to keep the CVA for each year "large enough" given a notional principal of 100 and rounding results to four digits.
3. This and other similar derivative-based strategies using "first generation" structured notes are discussed in Smith (1989).
4. This phenomenon of negative duration on a floating-rate note is examined in further detail in Smith (2006) and in Smith (2014). A closed-form equation for the modified duration of the floater is derived whereby the relevant interest rate is the yield on an otherwise comparable fixed-rate bond.

Chapter IV

Valuing Fixed-Income Bonds Having Embedded Call and Put Options

The binomial forward rate tree model is used in this chapter to illustrate some aspects of how an embedded option impacts the value of a fixed-income debt security.[1] This embedded option can be a *call option* in which the issuer is able to *buy* the bond back from the investor at a preset price (the call price) on preset dates (the call schedule) or it can be a *put option* in which the investor is able to *sell* the bond back to the issuer at a preset price on preset dates. A callable bond offers flexibility to the bond issuer to manage its liabilities by exercising the embedded option when its cost of borrowed funds goes down. A putable bond provides protection to the investor if yields in general rise, perhaps due to higher expected inflation. The investor can sell the bond back to the issuer and reinvest the proceeds at the new higher interest rate. The chapter starts with a callable bond; an example of a putable bond is included in the Study Questions in Section IV.5.

IV.1: Valuing an Embedded Call Option

The example in this section is a callable, 5%, annual coupon payment, 5-year corporate bond. The first step is to calculate the VND and

Exhibit IV-1: Valuation of a 5.00%, 5-Year, Non-Callable, Annual Coupon Payment Corporate Bond Using CVA

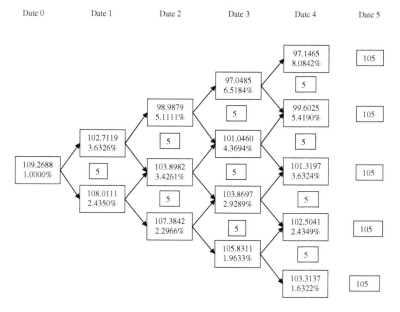

Credit Risk Parameters: 2.50% Conditional Probability of Default, 40% Recovery Rate

Date	Expected Exposure	LGD	POD	Discount Factor	CVA
1	110.3615	66.2169	2.50000%	0.990099	1.6390
2	108.5421	65.1253	2.43750%	0.960978	1.5255
3	107.2033	64.3220	2.37656%	0.928023	1.4186
4	106.0503	63.6302	2.31715%	0.894344	1.3186
5	105.0000	63.0000	2.25922%	0.860968	1.2254
			11.89043%		7.1272

Fair Value = 109.2688 − 7.1272 = 102.1416

CVA for the bond assuming that it is non-callable. This is shown in Exhibit IV-1. The VND is 109.2688 (per 100 of par value); the premium price reflects the coupon rate being higher than 3.00% on the benchmark bond trading at par value. The CVA is 7.1272, based on the assumed conditional default probability of 2.50% and a recovery rate of 40% for a loss severity of 60% for each year. This relatively high default probability suggests that this is a high-yield, non-investment-grade issuer. The cumulative probability of default over the 5-year time to maturity is 11.89043%. The fair value of the non-callable corporate bond is 102.1416 (=109.2688 − 7.1272).

The second step is to transform the CVA into an annual credit spread. Here the credit spread, denoted C-spread, is the uniform addition to the 1-year rates in the binomial forward rate tree such that the Date-0 price turns out to be the known fair value of 102.1416. The C-spread of 153.67 basis points is found by trial-and-error search, as presented in Exhibit IV-2. For example, at the Date-4 node where the 1-year benchmark rate is 8.0842%, the value of the bond is 95.7847:

$$\frac{105}{1 + 0.080842 + 0.015367} = 95.7847$$

Exhibit IV-2: Valuation of a 5.00%, 5-Year, Non-Callable, Annual Coupon Payment Corporate Bond Using the C-Spread

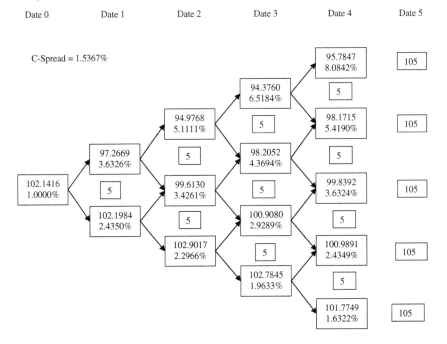

At the Date-1 node where the 1-year rate is 3.6326%, the value is 97.2669:

$$\frac{5 + (0.50 * 94.9768 + 0.50 * 99.6130)}{1 + 0.036326 + 0.015367} = 97.2669$$

The idea is that the credit risk on bond is represented by either the CVA of 7.1272 in terms of a present value on Date 0 or as a 5-year annual spread of 153.67 basis points. The advantage of modeling the credit spread is that it can be used to project the future bond prices that are necessary to determine the value of the embedded call option at each node in the tree. The critical and simplifying assumption is that this credit spread over the benchmark rate is constant over the five years. Therefore, the model captures only part of the call option value to the issuer — and the risk to the investor. In reality, the bond issuer will be able to exercise the call option if either the benchmark yield *or* the credit spread over the benchmark is lower, or some combination of the two factors. Therefore, holding the credit spread constant underestimates the actual call option value.

The binomial forward rate tree model also would underestimate the value of an embedded put option to the investor — and the risk to the issuer. The investor benefits from the option to sell the bond back to the issuer. This benefit arises from a combination of benchmark yields going up and the credit spread widening. This model has only one source of volatility and that is the benchmark 1-year rate. It would take a more complex model to factor in both volatility in the market interest rate and in the credit spread, and the interaction between them. To keep the model simple, the credit spread is assumed to be constant in this analysis.

Given the assumption of a constant credit spread, the value of the callable bond is calculated in Exhibit IV-3. The call schedule for this bond is indicated below the tree. The bond is first callable on Date 2 at par value (100), and then at the same price on Dates 3 and 4. The investor has call protection on Date 1. The model is general and can handle any pattern for the call prices and dates. For instance, the

Exhibit IV-3: Valuation of a 5%, 5-Year, Callable, Annual Coupon Payment Corporate Bond

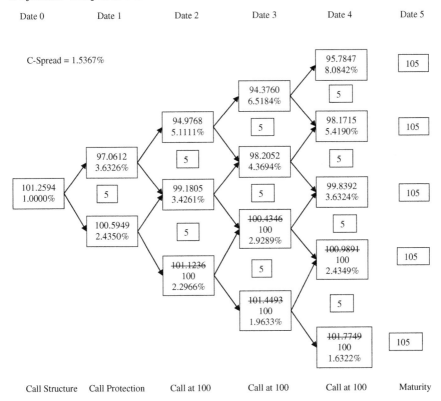

Date 0	Date 1	Date 2	Date 3	Date 4	Date 5
Call Structure	Call Protection	Call at 100	Call at 100	Call at 100	Maturity

call price sometimes is set at a premium above par value on the first call date and then declines to par as the maturity nears.

To see how the embedded call option is handled via backward induction, consider first the Date-4 possibilities. At the top of the tree where the 1-year rate is relatively high and the bond price is below par value, the issuer would not exercise the option to buy at 100. However, at the bottom two nodes where the rates are 2.4349% and 1.6322%, the bond would trade at a premium above par value. Clearly, the issuer would exercise the call option, so those prices are crossed out and replaced by the call price of 100. This reduction in

potential value represents the call risk to the investor and the benefit
to the issuer.

Now consider the Date-3 valuations. At the bottom of the tree
where the 1-year rate is 1.9633%, the bond value is 101.4493 before
considering the call option.

$$\frac{5 + (0.50 * 100 + 0.50 * 100)}{1 + 0.019633 + 0.015367} = 101.4493$$

Notice that the revised Date-4 values that register the exercise of
the call option are used in this calculation. The obtained value of
101.4493 is now crossed out and replaced with 100 because it is
assumed that the issuer exercises the option to buy the bond back
at the call price of 100 on Date 3. At the node above where the
1-year rate is 2.9289%, the value is also above par and the option is
exercised. It is "out of the money" at the two nodes at the top of the
tree for that date.

On Date 2, the option is "in the money" only at the lowest node
where the 1-year rate is 2.2966%. Its value would be 101.1236:

$$\frac{5 + (0.50 * 100 + 0.50 * 100)}{1 + 0.022966 + 0.015367} = 101.1236$$

Once again, the bond would be called, so the value is crossed out and
replaced by 100 (or whatever is the call price for that date). Continu-
ing with backward induction produces a Date-0 price of 101.2594 for
the callable bond. Therefore, the implied value of the embedded call
option is 0.8822 (per 100 of par value): $102.1416 - 101.2594 = 0.8822$.
It is inferred by the value of the otherwise equivalent non-callable
bond less the value of the callable bond.

IV.2: Calculating the Option-Adjusted Spread (OAS)

The option-adjusted spread is a statistic that is commonly used to
assess callable bonds. Suppose that a fixed-income investor seeks to
identify relative value among a series of callable bonds, for instance,
bonds from the same issuer (or issuers that are very similar with

respect to credit risk). Their call features differ in terms of call dates and prices. One of the bonds under consideration is the 5%, 5-year, callable bond that has a market price of 101.2594 per 100 of par value. The analyst calculates the Z-spread on the bond to be 1.73681%, the solution for Z in this expression:

$$101.2594 = \frac{5}{(1 + 0.010000 + Z)^1} + \frac{5}{(1 + 0.020101 + Z)^2}$$

$$+ \frac{5}{(1 + 0.025212 + Z)^3} + \frac{5}{(1 + 0.028310 + Z)^4}$$

$$+ \frac{105}{(1 + 0.030392 + Z)^5}$$

The benchmark spot rates are from Exhibit I-3.

The problem for the analyst in comparing Z-spreads for the various bonds is that they contain the embedded call option values — and those values will differ if the call dates and prices differ. The objective of OAS analysis is to extract the call option values from the Z-spreads. Suppose that the option value is determined to be 0.8822 per 100 of par value using a pricing model (for instance, the binomial tree model used in this exposition) and, most importantly, an assumption about benchmark yield volatility (for instance, 20%). Also, implicit in this calculation are assumptions about the credit risk parameters of the issuer of the callable bond.

Given that option value, the analyst estimates the *option-adjusted price* to be 102.1416, the *observed* price on the callable bond of 101.2594 plus the *estimated* value of the embedded call option of 0.8822 (per 100 of par value). The *option-adjusted yield* is 4.5120%, the solution for Y in this expression.

$$102.1416 = \frac{5}{(1 + Y)^1} + \frac{5}{(1 + Y)^2} + \frac{5}{(1 + Y)^3}$$

$$+ \frac{5}{(1 + Y)^4} + \frac{105}{(1 + Y)^5}$$

The *option-adjusted spread* is 1.53707%, the solution for OAS in this expression.

$$102.1416 = \frac{5}{(1 + 0.010000 + \text{OAS})^1} + \frac{5}{(1 + 0.020101 + \text{OAS})^2}$$
$$+ \frac{5}{(1 + 0.025212 + \text{OAS})^3} + \frac{5}{(1 + 0.028310 + \text{OAS})^4}$$
$$+ \frac{105}{(1 + 0.030392 + \text{OAS})^5}$$

It is no surprise that the OAS of 153.707 basis points is very close to the C-spread of 153.670 basis points, which is calculated above. The OAS and the C-spread are both spreads over benchmark yields assuming there is no embedded call option. The slight difference arises because the OAS as defined here is with respect to the benchmark spot curve and the C-spread is with respect to the 1-year benchmark rates in the binomial tree. In fact, some fixed-income authors define the OAS to be what is here the C-Spread.

A fixed-income investor would seek to identify the callable bond having the highest OAS. That bond would have the best relative value assuming the credit risks (and liquidity and taxation) are the same.

IV.3: Effective Duration and Convexity of a Callable Bond

A callable bond is an example of a debt security for which only effective duration and convexity are meaningful risk statistics, even though in practice yield durations and convexities are often reported by data services. Exhibit IV-4 shows the calculations for the 5-year, 5% callable bond. This bond has a fair value of 101.2594 in Exhibit IV-3 (or, 101.25943047 with greater precision for use as MV_0), based on the key assumptions — 20% volatility, 2.50% conditional default probability, and 40% recovery for each year.

The same steps as discussed in Sections IV.1 are used to get MV_+ and MV_- for the 5-basis-point shifts to the benchmark par curve.

Exhibit IV-4: Effective Duration and Convexity of a Callable Bond
5-Year, Callable, Annual Payment Callable Bond

	Fair Value	C-Spread
MV_0	101.25943047	1.53670%
MV_+	101.07215308	1.53744%
MV_-	101.44724990	1.53595%

Credit Risk Parameters: 2.50% Default Probability, 40% Recovery Rate

$$\text{Effective Duration} = \frac{101.44724990 - 101.07215308}{2 * 0.0005 * 101.25943047} = 3.7043$$

$$\text{Effective Convexity} = \frac{101.44724990 + 101.07215308 - (2 * 101.25943047)}{(0.0005)^2 * 101.25943047} = 21.4143$$

The shifted curves used in the calculation are from Exhibits II-9 and II-11 in Chapter II. First, fair values are obtained for an otherwise comparable non-callable bond, which gives the value for credit risk in the form of the CVA as of Date 0. Then, those fair values are used to get the C-spreads, which are the uniform additions to the 1-year rates in the binomial tree such that the same fair value is obtained. Note that in Exhibit IV-4 the C-spreads are slightly different for the three trees due to the slight difference in expected exposures to default loss. Finally, the specific terms of the call structure (first callable at par value on Date 2 and then on each coupon payment date until maturity) are used to get the projected bond values throughout the binomial tree. The fair values for the callable bond are calculated via backward induction after inserting the call price at the nodes where the option is exercised.

The effective duration and convexity for the 5%, 5-year callable bond are reported in Exhibit IV-4 to be 3.7043 and 21.4143, respectively. These statistics are lower than 4.4686 and 25.0045 on a 5%, 5-year non-callable bond (not exhibited) having the same credit risk parameters. The relationship between the two is illustrated in Exhibit IV-5. The non-callable has a higher market value for each

Exhibit IV-5: Relationship between a Callable Bond and a Non-Callable Bond

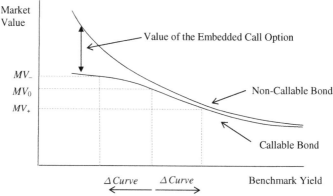

benchmark bond yield; the vertical difference between the two curves is the value of the embedded call option. It is small when the benchmark yield is high and increases as the yield goes down, indicating the benefit to the issuer in being able to buy back the bond and refinance the debt at a lower cost of funds. Note that the callable bond modeled here is a special case in that the credit spread is assumed to remain constant. Therefore, the value of the call option reflects only the probability that benchmark rates come down and not that the credit spread narrows.

The slopes of the curves in Exhibit IV-5 represent the effective duration statistics. The slope of the non-callable bond is steeper than the callable throughout the diagram, indicating higher duration and greater price sensitivity for a given change in the benchmark yield. The change in the slope represents the effective convexity. For the non-callable, it is always increasing and getting steeper as the benchmark yield is reduced. The price increase when the yield is lowered always exceeds (in absolute value) the price decrease when the yield is raised by the same amount. That describes the *positive convexity* of a traditional fixed-income bond having no embedded options. However, for the callable bond, the change in the slope can be quite different. At some low yield, there is an inflection point and the convexity becomes negative.

This equation for effective convexity restates equation (12) in Chapter II, changing the numerator to focus on the sign of the statistic.

$$\text{Effective Convexity} = \frac{[(MV_-) - (MV_0)] - [(MV_0) - (MV_+)]}{(\Delta \text{Curve})^2 * (MV_0)}$$

(1)

In Exhibit IV-5 negative convexity is evident in that $[(MV_-) - (MV_0)]$ is pictured to be less than $[(MV_0) - (MV_+)]$, therefore the numerator would be negative. In essence, the embedded call option puts a limit on price appreciation associated with lower benchmark interest rates.

IV.4: The Impact of a Change in Volatility on the Callable Bond

The presence of the embedded call option makes the value of a callable bond particularly sensitive to the assumed level of interest rate volatility. A long position (indicated by the "+" sign) in a callable bond can be interpreted as buying a non-callable bond and writing a standalone call option (indicated by the "−" sign):

$$+\text{Callable Bond} = +\text{Non-callable Bond} - \text{Call Option} \qquad (2)$$

Similarly, issuing a callable bond is like issuing a non-callable and buying the call option:

$$-\text{Callable Bond} = -\text{Non-callable Bond} + \text{Call Option} \qquad (3)$$

Lower volatility reduces the value of the call option because there are fewer circumstances when the bond value exceeds the call price. That raises the value of the callable bond, benefiting the investor at the expense of the bond issuer.

This result is demonstrated by comparing the results for the 5%, 5-year callable bond for 10% volatility to those for 20% volatility. This 10% volatility tree is from Exhibit II-6. The first step again is to obtain the fair value of an otherwise equivalent 5%, 5-year

Exhibit IV-6: Valuation of a 5.00%, 5-Year, Non-Callable, Annual Coupon Payment Corporate Bond Using CVA for 10% Volatility

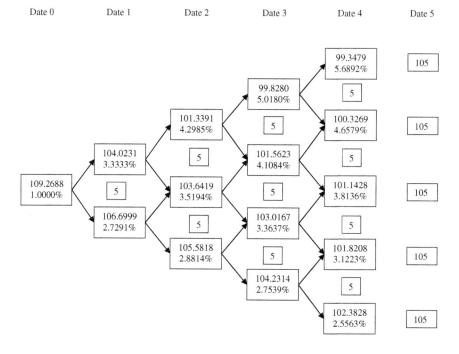

| Date 0 | Date 1 | Date 2 | Date 3 | Date 4 | Date 5 |

Credit Risk Parameters: 2.50% Conditional Probability of Default, 40% Recovery Rate

Date	Expected Exposure	LGD	POD	Discount Factor	CVA
1	110.3615	66.2169	2.50000%	0.990099	1.6390
2	108.5512	65.1307	2.43750%	0.960978	1.5256
3	107.2245	64.3347	2.37656%	0.928023	1.4189
4	106.0737	63.6442	2.31715%	0.894344	1.3189
5	105.0000	63.0000	2.25922%	0.860968	1.2254
			11.89043%		7.1279

Fair Value = 109.2688 − 7.1279 = 102.1409

non-callable bond. This is done in Exhibit IV-6 for 10% volatility — the VND is 109.2688, the CVA is 7.1279, and the fair value is 102.1409 (=109.2688 − 7.1279). In Exhibit IV-1 for 20% volatility, the VND is the same at 109.2688, but the CVA is slightly lower at 7.1272 because volatility impacts the expected exposure, leading to a slightly higher fair value of 102.1416. This provides another example of the volatility effect on the value of a traditional bond not having an embedded option that is discussed in Section II-3 of Chapter II.

The second step is to solve for the C-Spread — the spread over each 1-year benchmark rate such that the Date-0 value is 102.1409. That turns out to be 1.53707% (the binomial tree corresponding to Exhibit IV-2 is not shown). As the change in volatility has only a small change in the bond value, it is no surprise that the change in C-spread is minor (1.53707% versus 1.53670%). This C-Spread is used to calculate the future values for the bond if it were non-callable. These values are then used to determine whether the bond is called on future dates by the issuer.

Exhibit IV-7 shows that the issuer calls the bond on Date 4 at the bottom two nodes where the rates are 3.1223% and 2.5563% because the values exceed the call price of 100. Those values are crossed out and replaced with the call price of 100. On Date 3 the bond is called only at the bottom node where the rate is 2.7539%. The bond would have been worth 100.6799 to the investor:

$$\frac{5 + (0.50 * 100 + 0.50 * 100)}{1 + 0.027539 + 0.0153707} = 100.6799$$

Note that the C-Spread is added to the benchmark rate to get the discounted value. Proceeding with backward induction obtains a Date-0 fair value of 101.8257 for 10% volatility.

The impact of the assumed volatility on the value of callable bond is summarized in the following table:

Volatility Assumption	Fair Value
10%, in Exhibit IV-7	101.8257
20%, in Exhibit IV-3	101.2594
Difference	0.5663

Exhibit IV-7: Valuation of a 5%, 5-Year, Annual Coupon Payment Callable Corporate Bond Using 10% Volatility

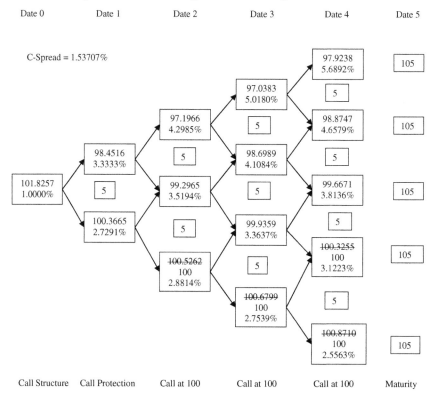

The reduction in volatility increases the value of the callable bond by 0.5663 per 100 of par value. It is important to remember that this binomial model, which tracks projected benchmark 1-year bond yields, captures only part of the value of the embedded call option because the credit spread is assumed to remain constant. In general, the issuer of the callable bond also benefits from a narrowing credit spread over the benchmark rate as that reduces the cost of refinancing the debt.

IV.5: Study Questions

(A) Calculate the fair value of a 4.25%, annual payment, 5-year, callable corporate bond assuming 20% volatility. The bond is callable by the issuer at 102 on Date 2, at 101 on Date 3, and at 100 on Date 4. The credit risk parameters for the corporate issuer are a conditional default probability of 1.25% and a recovery rate of 30% for each year.

(B) Calculate the fair value of a 3.50%, annual payment, 5-year, putable corporate bond assuming 20% volatility. The bond is putable by the investor at par value on Dates 2, 3, and 4. The

Exhibit IV-8: Valuation of a 4.25%, 5-Year, Non-Callable, Annual Coupon Payment Corporate Bond Using CVA

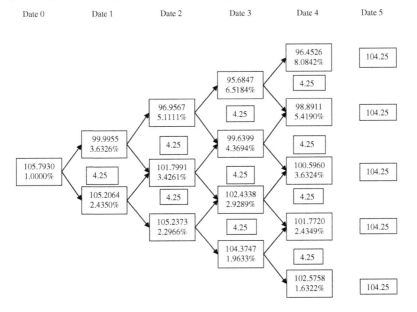

Credit Risk Parameters: 1.25% Conditional Probability of Default, 30% Recovery Rate

Date	Expected Exposure	LGD	POD	Discount Factor	CVA
1	106.8510	74.7957	1.25000%	0.990099	0.9257
2	105.6981	73.9886	1.23438%	0.960978	0.8777
3	105.0350	73.5245	1.21895%	0.928023	0.8317
4	104.5785	73.2050	1.20371%	0.894344	0.7881
5	104.2500	72.9750	1.18866%	0.860968	0.7468
			6.09569%		4.1700

Fair Value = 105.7930 − 4.1700 = 101.6231

credit risk parameters for the corporate issuer are a conditional default probability of 1.00% and a recovery rate of 40% for each year.

IV.6: Answers to the Study Questions

(A) The first step in the valuation process is to get the fair value of the 4.25%, annual payment, 5-year bond assuming that it is non-callable. Given the credit risk parameters, that fair value is shown in Exhibit IV-8 to be 101.6231 per 100 of par value. The second step is to solve by trial and error for the C-Spread, which is the uniform addition to the 1-year benchmark rates such that the fair value of the bond rounds off to 101.6231. The C-Spread turns out to be 0.90204%, shown in Exhibit IV-9. The key point is that the credit risk is captured by a CVA of 4.1700 in terms of a present value on Date 0 or as an annual spread of 0.90204%.

Exhibit IV-9: Valuation of a 4.25%, 5-Year, Non-Callable, Annual Coupon Payment Corporate Bond Using the C-Spread

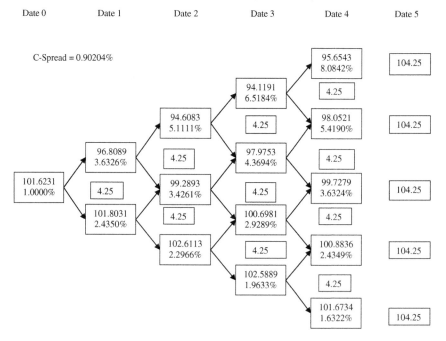

Exhibit IV-10: Valuation of a 4.25%, 5-Year, Callable, Annual Coupon Payment Corporate Bond

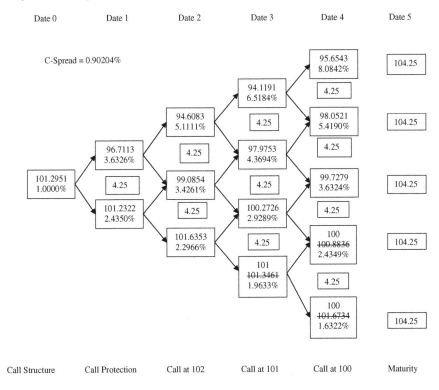

Both numbers reflect the assumed annual default probability of 1.25% and a recovery rate of 30%.

Exhibit IV-10 shows that the fair value of the callable bond is 101.2951 under the strong assumption of constant credit risk. The value of the embedded call option is calculated to be 0.3280 (=101.6231 − 101.2951). Constant credit risk implies that the issuer will only exercise the call option if benchmark interest rates are sufficiently low. This valuation approach neglects the possibility that the credit spread narrows by enough to allow the issuer to refinance the debt at a lower cost of funds even if benchmark rates are steady or even rise.

The corporate issuer exercises the option on Date 4 at the bottom two nodes where the benchmark rates are 2.4349% and

1.6322%. On Date 3 the option to buy back the bond at 101 is exercised only if the benchmark rate is 1.9633% because the value of 101.3461 (calculated using the Date 4 values of 100, which replace the original values) exceeds the call price of 101. The option would not be exercised on Date 2 because the values are less than the call price of 102.

(B) The first two steps to value the 3.50%, annual payment, 5-year putable bond are the same as the callable bond in (A). The VND for the bond is 102.3172 and the CVA is 2.8128 given

Exhibit IV-11: Valuation of a 3.50%, 5-Year, Non-Putable, Annual Coupon Payment Corporate Bond Using CVA

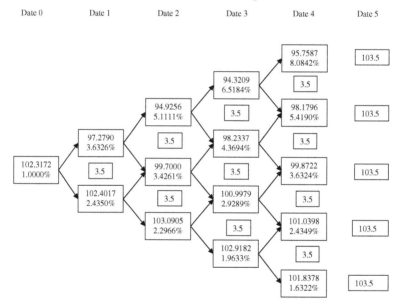

Credit Risk Parameters: 1.00% Conditional Probability of Default, 40% Recovery Rate

Date	Expected Exposure	LGD	POD	Discount Factor	CVA
1	103.3404	62.0042	1.00000%	0.990099	0.6139
2	102.8540	61.7124	0.99000%	0.960978	0.5871
3	102.8667	61.7200	0.98010%	0.928023	0.5614
4	103.1067	61.8640	0.97030%	0.894344	0.5368
5	103.5000	62.1000	0.96060%	0.860968	0.5136
			4.90100%		2.8128

Fair Value = 102.3172 − 2.8128 = 99.5044

Exhibit IV-12: Valuation of a 3.50%, 5-Year, Non-Putable, Annual Coupon Payment Corporate Bond Using the C-Spread

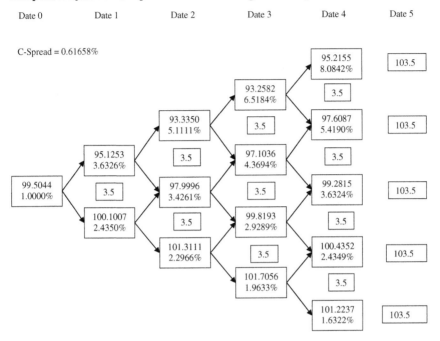

a conditional probability of default of 1.00% and a recovery rate of 40% for each year. The fair value of the bond if it were non-putable (and, of course, non-callable) is 99.5044 (=102.3172−2.8128) as shown in Exhibit IV-11. The C-Spread is 0.61658%. Exhibit IV-12 shows that with this uniform addition to the benchmark rates in the binomial tree also results in a fair value of 99.5044.

A putable bond provides value to the bondholder when benchmark rates are high so that bond values are less than the put price of 100. The investor can sell the bond back to the issuer to capture that difference. Therefore, it is no surprise that the put option is exercised at nodes in the top of the tree in Exhibit IV-13. The option is exercised at the top three nodes on Date 4 and the top two on Dates 2 and 3. In each case the bond value is replaced with 100 and the backward induction procedure

Exhibit IV-13: Valuation of a 3.50%, 5-Year, Putable, Annual Coupon Payment Corporate Bond

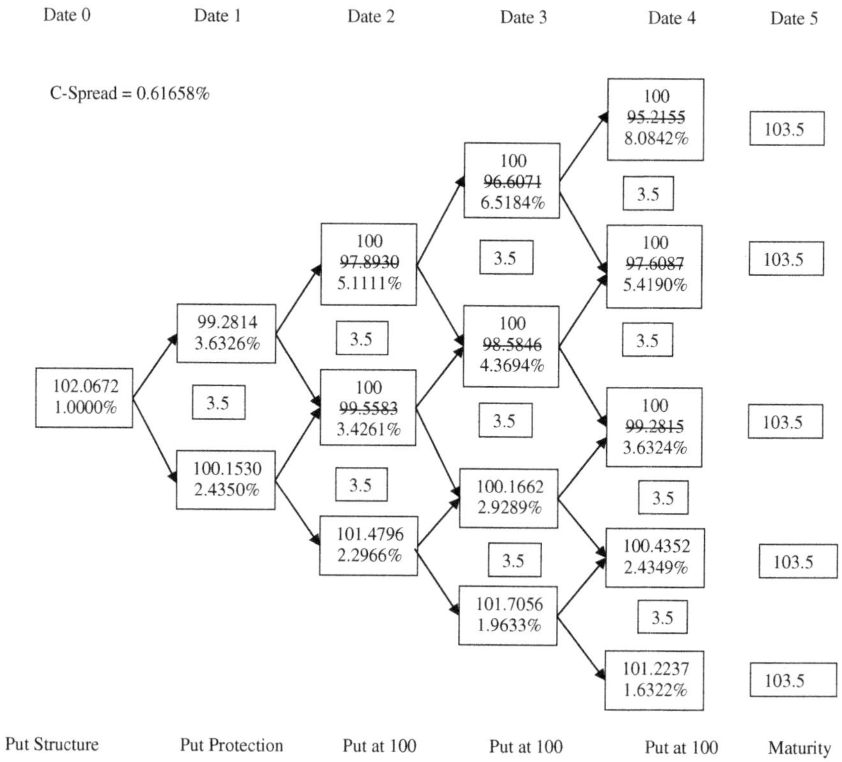

Date 0	Date 1	Date 2	Date 3	Date 4	Date 5

C-Spread = 0.61658%

Put Structure	Put Protection	Put at 100	Put at 100	Put at 100	Maturity

proceeds. The fair value of the putable bond is 102.0672. The value of the embedded option is 2.5628 (=102.0672 − 99.5044). As with the call option, this value is understated because of the assumption of a constant credit spread. In this case, the holder of the putable bond could also benefit from a widening credit spread. The bond price might even dip below par value (motivating the option to sell the bond back to the issuer) even if benchmark yields are steady or fall.

Endnote

1. A different approach to using the binomial model to include default risk and embedded options is presented in Finnerty (1999).

Chapter V

Valuing Interest Rate Swaps
with CVA and DVA

The valuation of an interest rate swap in a world of XVA is particularly important because credit risk is *bilateral* on this type of derivative contract, unlike the *unilateral* credit risk on a debt security or an interest rate cap or floor. At issuance, the typical interest rate swap has a value of zero; it is known as an *at-market* or *par* swap. Subsequently, as time passes and as market rates change, the value of the swap becomes positive to one of the two counterparties and negative to the other. It is also possible for the value of the swap to change sign during its lifetime — what was once an asset can switch on a future date to the other side of the balance sheet to become a liability, and vice versa. Therefore, both the CVA (the credit risk of the counterparty) and the DVA (the party's own credit risk) matter in valuation. Another of the XVA, in particular, the FVA (the funding valuation adjustment) is addressed in the next chapter.

A general relationship for the fair value of an interest rate swap, neglecting the others in the collection of XVA (in particular, the LVA, TVA, and FVA), is:

$$\text{Value}^{\text{SWAP}} = \text{VND} - \text{CVA} + \text{DVA} \tag{1}$$

As in the previous chapters, VND is the value assuming no default, CVA is the credit valuation adjustment, and DVA is the debit (or debt) valuation adjustment. The VND for the swap is calculated using the binomial forward rate tree for the 1-year benchmark bond yield and can be a positive or negative amount. This forward rate tree is shown in Exhibit I-1 in Chapter I and, importantly, assumes constant volatility, here 20% per year. The tree is based on the par curve for the benchmark bonds given in Exhibit I-2 and the discount factors, spot rates, and forward rates in Exhibit I-3.

V.1: A 3% Fixed-Rate Interest Rate Swap

Exhibit V-1 displays a plain vanilla interest rate swap exchanging a fixed rate of 3% for the 1-year benchmark bond rate. The payer of the fixed rate is known as "the payer"; the fixed-rate receiver is the "the receiver". The designated name of the counterparty follows the fixed-rate leg of the exchange. The 1-year benchmark bond rate, known as the *reference rate* to the contract, is exchanged (or swapped) with the fixed rate each period. This 5-year, 3% interest rate swap has a notional principal of 100 and entails five annual net settlement payments in cash in arrears. If the 1-year rate is determined to be 8.0842%, the receiver owes the payer 5.0842 at the end of the year: $(0.080842 - 0.0300) * 100 = 5.0842$. If the 1-year rate is 1.6322%, the payer owes the receiver 1.3678: $(0.0300 - 0.016322) * 100 = 1.3678$. These net settlement payments are made at the end of the period (in arrears, as with floating-rate notes). In general, the payment is adjusted by the day-count factor — interest rate swaps are usually settled quarterly or semiannually. Sometimes, there is a different day-count convention for the floating-rate leg of the swap than for the fixed-rate leg, for instance, actual/360 for the money market reference rate and actual/actual or 30/360 for the fixed rate. The

Exhibit V-1: "Plain Vanilla" Fixed-for-Floating Interest Rate Swap on the 1-Year Benchmark Bond Rate

examples here are for annual settlement based on the 1-year rate, so the day-count factor is always one.

The VND for the 5-year, 3% swap is zero for both counterparties. The binomial tree establishing this result is shown in Exhibit V-2 from the perspective of the fixed-rate receiver and in Exhibit V-3 from the perspective of the payer. All of the projected net settlement payments, which are placed across from the nodes in the tree, and the swap values in Exhibits V-2 and V-3 are the same in absolute value. The *receiver swap* in Exhibit V-2 has positive values and payments in the lower part of the tree — at those nodes for which the 3% fixed rate is higher than the 1-year benchmark reference rates — and negative values and payments in the top part. All of the signs are reversed in Exhibit V-3 for the *payer swap*. The fixed-rate payer has positive values and payments when the 1-year benchmark rate that is received exceeds the 3% fixed rate that is paid. An interest

Exhibit V-2: Valuation of a 3.00%, 5-Year, Receive-Fixed Interest Rate Swap Assuming No Default

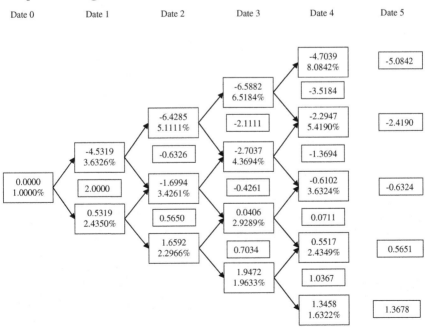

Exhibit V-3: Valuation of a 3.00%, 5-Year, Pay-Fixed Interest Rate Swap Assuming No Default

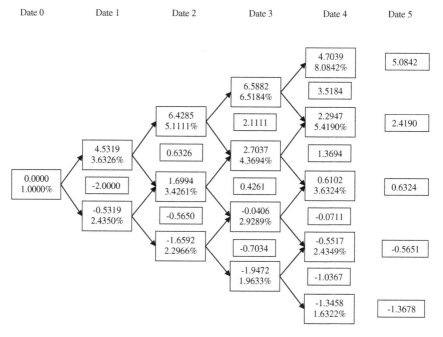

rate swap is an archetype for a *zero-sum game* in that all the gains to one party are offset by the losses to the counterparty.

Because there are both positive and negative amounts in the tree, the swap value calculations require some attention. For example, in Exhibit V-2 on Date 2 when the 1-year rate is 3.4261%, the value of the swap to the receiver is −1.6994:

$$\frac{-0.4261 + [(0.50 * -2.7037) + (0.050 * 0.0406)]}{1.034261} = -1.6994$$

The first term in the numerator, −0.4261, is the projected settlement payment owed by the receiver to the counterparty at the end of the year on Date 3 because the reference rate exceeds the 3% fixed rate: $(0.0300 - 0.034261) * 100 = -0.4261$. The second term is the expected value of the swap on Date 3 given the 50–50 odds of the 1-year rate going up to 4.3694%, which leads to negative value for the swap (−2.7037), and going down to 2.9289%, which leads to a positive value (0.0406). Those amounts are discounted back to Date 2 using 3.4261% as the discount rate. Proceeding with backward induction through the tree produces a Date-0 value of zero for the swap, assuming no default.

This VND of zero for the 5-year, 3% interest rate swap is not a coincidence. The 5-year, annual payment, benchmark bond underlying the binomial tree is priced at par value and has a coupon rate of 3%; see Exhibit I-2. Also, a 5-year floating-rate note that pays the 1-year benchmark rate flat would be priced at par value. One of the classic interpretations of an interest rate swap is that, neglecting counterparty credit risk, its cash flows are the same as a *long/short* combination of a fixed-rate bond that pays the swap rate and a floating-rate note that pays the reference rate flat. To the fixed-rate receiver, the swap is the same as buying the fixed-rate bond, financed by issuing the floater. To the fixed-rate payer, the swap is a combination of a long position in the floating-rate note and a short position in the fixed-rate bond. The net cash flows on the combination produce the same values and payments as in Exhibits V-2 and V-3. The caveat, however, is "neglecting counterparty credit risk". The introduction of bilateral credit risk and the CVA and DVA complicates this interpretation, as illustrated in the examples in this chapter.

Suppose that the counterparties to the swap are financial institutions, in particular, money-center commercial banks that are active dealers in derivatives markets. The conditional probability of default for both entities is assumed arbitrarily to be 0.50% for each year.[1] Also, the recovery rate is assumed to be just 10%, giving a loss severity of 90% if default by the bank were to occur. The low recovery rate is chosen to reflect the junior status of derivatives counterparties in the priority of claim — deposits are more senior than swaps. The swap for now is taken to be unsecured — the effects of collateralization and central clearing, which have become standard for inter-dealer derivative transactions, is discussed in the next section. The CVA and DVA calculations are shown in Exhibit V-4. The CVA/DVA for the fixed-rate payer (the present value of the expected loss suffered

Exhibit V-4: CVA and DVA Calculations on the 3.00%, 5-Year, Interest Rate Swap

Credit Risk of the Fixed-Rate Payer

Credit Risk Parameters: 0.50% Conditional Probability of Default, 10% Recovery Rate

Date	Expected Exposure	LGD	POD	Discount Factor	CVA/DVA
1	1.2660	1.1394	0.50000%	0.990099	0.0056
2	0.5561	0.5004	0.49750%	0.960978	0.0024
3	0.3986	0.3587	0.49501%	0.928023	0.0016
4	0.4253	0.3828	0.49254%	0.894344	0.0017
5	0.2268	0.2041	0.49007%	0.860968	0.0009
			2.47512%		0.0122

Credit Risk of the Fixed-Rate Receiver

Credit Risk Parameters: 0.50% Conditional Probability of Default, 10% Recovery Rate

Date	Expected Exposure	LGD	POD	Discount Factor	CVA/DVA
1	1.2660	1.1394	0.50000%	0.990099	0.0056
2	2.6319	2.3687	0.49750%	0.960978	0.0113
3	2.5770	2.3193	0.49501%	0.928023	0.0107
4	2.1708	1.9537	0.49254%	0.894344	0.0086
5	1.1597	1.0437	0.49007%	0.860968	0.0044
			2.47512%		0.0406

by the receiver if the payer defaults) is 0.0122 per 100 of notional principal; the CVA/DVA for the fixed-rate receiver (the loss suffered by the payer if the receiver defaults) is 0.0406.

Including the credit risk adjustments, the 3% swap turns out to be an asset to the fixed-rate receiver and a liability to the payer. Even though the VND is zero, the difference in the credit risks of the two counterparties drives this result. The swap values are based on equation (1).

To the fixed-rate receiver:

$$\text{Value}^{\text{SWAP}} = 0.0000 - 0.0122 + 0.0406 = +0.0284$$

To the fixed-rate payer:

$$\text{Value}^{\text{SWAP}} = 0.0000 - 0.0406 + 0.0122 = -0.0284$$

To the fixed-rate receiver, the CVA is the credit risk of the payer (0.0122) and the DVA is its own credit risk (0.0406). To the fixed-rate payer, the CVA is the credit risk of the receiver (0.0406) and the DVA is its own risk (0.0122). An important observation is that this imbalance in credit risk occurs even though the counterparties are assumed to have the same probability of default and the same recovery rate. The imbalance arises because of the difference in their *expected exposures* to default loss for each future date—and that is due to the shape of the underlying yield curve.

The calculation of the expected exposures involves a key decision about modeling credit risk, namely, what to do about the negative values and payments in the binomial tree. Most derivative contracts in practice are documented under an ISDA (International Swap and Derivatives Association) master agreement that contains a provision for *closeout netting*. This means that if there is a default, all the derivatives with the defaulting counterparty are combined so that positive values (assets that are exposed to loss) can be offset by negative values. For instance, suppose that the fixed-rate payer defaults on Date 4. Clearly, the fixed-rate receiver is exposed to loss for the positive values and payments in the lower portion of the tree in Exhibit V-2. In principle, if the swap is part of a derivatives portfolio covered by a master agreement, the negative values at the top of the tree diminish the overall exposure because they could be used to "absorb" losses on another contract. An example of closeout netting for two swaps is included in the Study Questions.

While the implications of closeout netting certainly matter to a risk manager, valuation in this chapter follows the accounting perspective and focuses on *exit value* as reported in financial statements. The exit value is the amount that would be received from selling an asset in an "orderly transaction" (meaning not a forced liquidation or distress sale) or paid to transfer or extinguish a liability. The exit value in principle should not be affected by other positions held by the seller of the security or the derivative contract that are not passed on to the buyer.

There is another netting effect even with a single swap contract. That can be called *value and payment* netting. If there is a default by the counterparty on a future date, the risk exposure to the non-defaulting party is the value of the swap on that date plus the net settlement payment that was determined on the previous date. Those

Exhibit V-5: Expected Exposure to the 3% Fixed-Rate Receiver if the Payer Defaults

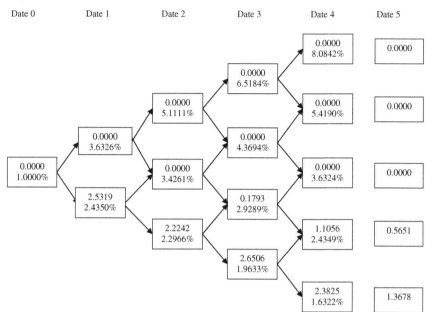

Date 0	Date 1	Date 2	Date 3	Date 4	Date 5

values and payments can be either positive or negative. What matters is the sum — a positive sum represents exposure, a negative sum does not. Therefore, negative amounts are converted to zeros in calculating the expected exposures in Exhibit V-4. This is illustrated in Exhibit V-5 for the exposure facing the fixed-rate receiver if the payer defaults and Exhibit V-6 for the payer's exposure if the receiver defaults.[2]

Consider first the risk exposure facing the fixed-rate receiver. This requires looking at the swap values and net settlement payments in Exhibit V-2, the expected exposure in the upper table in Exhibit V-4, and the exposures in Exhibit V-5. By assumption, the probability of default on Date 0 is zero, so there is no default risk. Moreover, the value of the swap is zero so even if default on that date were to be allowed, the exposure is still zero. On Date 1, the 1-year benchmark rate could go "down" to 2.4350% where the swap value is +0.5319. The fixed-rate receiver also is scheduled to receive a net settlement

Exhibit V-6: Expected Exposure to the 3% Fixed-Rate Payer if the Receiver Defaults

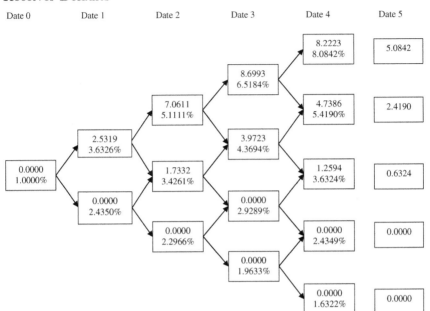

payment of 2.0000 on Date 1. Therefore, the combined exposure is 2.5319(= 0.5319 + 2.0000). If instead the benchmark rate goes up to 3.6326%, the swap value is −4.5319. Combined with the positive settlement payment, the exposure is −2.5319(= −4.5319 + 2.0000). That converts to zero in Exhibit V-5. Given the equal probabilities of the rate rising and falling, the *expected* exposure for Date 1 shown in Exhibit V-4 is 1.2660:(0.50 ∗ 0) + (0.50 ∗ 2.5319) = 1.2660. [Recall that all calculations are carried out on a spreadsheet that preserves precision and rounded results are reported.]

For Date 2 and the benchmark rate of 5.1111%, the swap value is −6.4285 and the payment −0.6326 (the receiver owes the settlement payment to the counterparty). The sum is negative so the risk exposure is zero. At the benchmark rate of 2.2966%, the swap value is +1.6592 and the payment is +0.5650. The exposure is the sum, +2.2242. The middle rate of 3.4261% is more complicated because the net payment could be either -0.6326 or $+0.5660$, with equal probabilities. The combined exposure is the swap value (-1.6994) plus the expected payment of $-0.0330 : (0.50 * -0.6326) + (0.50 * +0.5650) = -0.0330$. These sum to a negative amount, so the exposure for that rate in the tree converts to zero. The overall expected exposure for Date 2 of 0.5561 in Exhibit V-4 uses the probabilities of arriving at each node in the tree: $(0.25 * 0) + (0.50 * 0) + (0.25 * 2.2242) = 0.5561$. The same steps are used for Dates 3 and 4. For Date 5, the expected exposure is just the probability-weighted final net settlements. The top three are converted to zeros because the scheduled payment is from the receiver to the payer.

The default risk facing the fixed-rate payer uses the swap values and net settlement payments in Exhibit V-3, the expected exposure in the lower table in Exhibit V-4, and the exposures in Exhibit V-6. These are the calculations for the risk exposures for Date 4, written as the maximum of zero and the sum of the swap value and the expected settlement payment:

At 8.0842%   Max $[0, 4.7039 + 3.5184] = 8.2223$
At 5.4190%   Max $[0, 2.2947 + (3.5184 + 1.3694)/2] = 4.7386$
At 3.6324%   Max $[0, 0.6102 + (1.3694 - 0.0711)/2] = 1.2594$
At 2.4349%   Max $[0, -0.5517 + (-0.0711 - 1.0367)/2] = 0$
At 1.6322%   Max $[0, -1.3458 - 1.0367] = 0$

The expected exposure for Date 4 is $2.1708 : (0.0625 * 8.2223) + (0.25 * 4.7386) + (0.375 * 1.2594) + (0.25 * 0) + (0.0625 * 0) = 2.1708$.

It is apparent that the expected exposures are much higher for default by the fixed-rate receiver than by the payer. The credit risk exposure facing the receiver arising from default by the payer is "front-loaded", centered on the (known) Date-1 settlement payment of 2 per 100 of notional principal owed by the payer. The credit risk exposure facing the fixed-rate payer due to default by the receiver is more "back-loaded" and significantly larger on future dates. The imbalance arises because of the upward slope of the benchmark yield curve and occurs even with equally risky counterparties in terms of their assumed default probabilities and loss severities.

V.2: The Effects of Collateralization

Suppose that the two financial institutions are negotiating the terms to enter a 5-year, at-market (or par), non-collateralized, interest rate swap. As just demonstrated, a fixed rate of 3% does not lead to an initial fair value of zero. The fixed rate needs to be lower because at 3% the receiver has a positive value (+0.0284) and the payer a negative value (−0.0284), after adjusting the VND of zero for credit risk. The requisite fixed rate can be obtained by trial-and-error search using the valuation model. It turns out that a fixed rate of 2.99378% produces a value that rounds to +0.0000 to the receiver and −0.0000 to the payer.

The VND for the receive-fixed swap goes down from zero for a 3% fixed rate to −0.0288 per 100 of notional principal for the fixed rate of 2.99378%. At the slightly lower fixed rate, the VND for the pay-fixed swap goes up from zero to +0.0288. The CVA/DVA for the payer becomes 0.0121 and 0.0409 for the receiver. The swap has an initial fair value of zero for both counterparties.

To the fixed-rate receiver:

$$\text{Value}^{\text{SWAP}} = -0.0288 - 0.0121 + 0.0409 = 0.0000$$

To the fixed-rate payer:

$$\text{Value}^{\text{SWAP}} = +0.0288 - 0.0409 + 0.0121 = 0.0000$$

A more likely scenario is that the two major financial institutions set the fixed rate at 3%, which produces a VND of zero, and then use collateralization (or central clearing) to reduce the CVA and DVA to approach zero.[3] Collateralization to minimize credit risk has been used in the interest rate swap market since the 1990s after the advent of the CSA (Credit Support Annex) to the standard ISDA document.

The typical CSA calls for a *zero threshold*, meaning that only the counterparty for which the swap has negative value posts collateral, which usually is cash but also can be qualifying highly marketable securities (such as Treasury bills, notes, and bonds). The CSA can be *one-way* (only the "weaker" counterparty is required to post collateral if the swap has negative value from its perspective) or *two-way* (both counterparties are obligated to post collateral when the value is negative). The threshold can be negative, meaning that a certain amount of collateral is posted even if the swap has zero or positive value. That provision makes the collateralization very similar to a margin account on an exchange-traded futures contract. The threshold also can be positive, meaning that the swap value has to reach a certain negative value before collateral is posted.

The Basel Committee on Banking Supervision now requires derivatives dealers to post "initial margin" on its non-centrally cleared contracts. This margin, sometimes called an independent amount, has the same effect as a negative threshold in the CSA. Subsequent postings of collateral as the market value of the derivative goes against the dealer are known as "variation margin." This regulation started in September 2016 for large dealers and is being phased in to cover all by 2020. Importantly, this leads to a new XVA called the MVA (margin valuation adjustment). The MVA is the present value of the future funding costs for the margin; see Ruiz (2016) for an approach to calculate the MVA using an XVA engine.

The impact of collateralization (and central clearing) can be modeled here with the assumed recovery rate. While the probability of default does not change, the presence of collateral equal to the fair value of the swap implies that the recovery rate approaches 100% and that the loss severity approaches zero. There could still be some residual risk with a zero (or even negative) threshold because the counterparty needing to post collateral typically has a few days to meet the requirement. Also, there is price risk on non-cash collateral even if the security is highly marketable. The swap valuation model and trial-and-error search produce the result that an assumed recovery rate of 99.89% for each counterparty gives a fair value that rounds off to 0.0000 for 5-year, 3% fixed rate contract, assuming the default probabilities remain at 0.50%.

The floating rate for the swaps in these examples is the 1-year benchmark government bond rate. In practice, the money market reference rate typically is 3-month LIBOR (in the U.S. dollar market), not just on swaps but also on interest rate caps and floors and floating-rate notes. This reality was largely inconsequential for modeling derivatives valuation prior to the financial crisis of 2007–09. The reference rate in the model such as in this book would be stated to be 12-month LIBOR. LIBOR discount factors as in Exhibit I-3, which are used to calculate the implied spot and forward rates, would be bootstrapped from a combination of bank time deposit rates, Eurodollar futures contracts, and interest rate swaps. In principle, the same binomial forward rate tree as in Exhibit I-1 could have been derived for 20% volatility.

The justification for treating LIBOR as the risk-free benchmark rate was that the spread between LIBOR and Treasury bill rates (known as the TED spread between Treasuries and Eurodollar time deposits) was fairly low and stable. That changed dramatically during and after the financial crisis when the TED spread widened and the implicit credit and liquidity risks on LIBOR time deposits (in particular, for the commercial banks that report the rates that comprise the LIBOR index) became a significant concern to market participants.

Since the financial crisis, the OIS swap rate (standing for Overnight Indexed Swap) has emerged as the new standard for the interbank risk-free rate.[4] An overnight indexed swap is a derivative contract on the total return of a low-risk reference rate that is compounded daily over a set time period. In the U.S., the daily effective fed funds rate is used. During the financial crisis, the LIBOR-OIS spread, which widened along with the TED spread, was widely watched as an indicator of bank credit and liquidity risk. Prior to August 2007, this spread was usually just 8–10 basis points but ballooned out to 350 basis points in September 2008.

The key point for derivatives valuation is that many interest rate swaps are now collateralized or centrally cleared. Therefore, counterparty credit risk is minimized and the discount factors used to obtain fair values should represent "risk-free" rates even though the "risky" LIBOR reference rate continues to be used to determine future net settlement payments. A more complete swap valuation model needs a *dual curve* approach — one forward curve to get the projected future rates given the assumed volatility and another curve for discounting, but that goes beyond the scope of this introduction to valuation. The examples to follow continue with the traditional *single curve* approach whereby the reference rates in the binomial forward rate tree that determine settlement payments on the swap are the same rates used to discount the cash flows.

V.3: An Off-Market, Seasoned 4.25% Fixed-Rate Interest Rate Swap

Suppose that several years ago a corporation entered a 4.25%, pay-fixed, non-collateralized interest rate swap against the 1-year benchmark rate with a commercial bank as the counterparty. The notional principal is 100 and the swap settles annually in arrears in cash on a net basis. A settlement payment has just been made and five years remain until maturity. The fair value of the swap, which is calculated below, is −5.6307 to the corporate fixed-rate payer and +5.6307 to the bank fixed-rate receiver. Fixed rates on 5-year swaps are now lower than when this derivative was initiated. In fact, the current fixed rate on a 5-year swap would be 3% before including the CVA and DVA of the counterparties. Therefore, the corporation is paying an above-market fixed rate of 4.25% for receipt of the reference rate on this *off-market* (or *non-par*), seasoned interest rate swap.

A straightforward method to obtain the VND for the swap is to discount the *annuity* representing the difference between the contractual and current swap market fixed rates, times the notional principal. This annuity is −1.25 : (0.0300 − 0.0425) * 100 = −1.25. The present value of the annuity is calculated using the benchmark bond discount factors from Exhibit I-3. The VND is −5.7930 from the perspective of the corporate payer of the fixed rate.

$$(-1.25 * 0.990099) + (-1.25 * 0.960978) + (-1.25 * 0.928023)$$
$$+ (-1.25 * 0.894344) + (-1.25 * 0.860968) = -5.7930$$

Another method to calculate the value assuming no default uses the binomial forward rate tree for 20% volatility, as demonstrated in

Exhibit V-7: Valuation of a 4.25%, 5-Year, Pay-Fixed Interest Rate Swap Assuming No Default

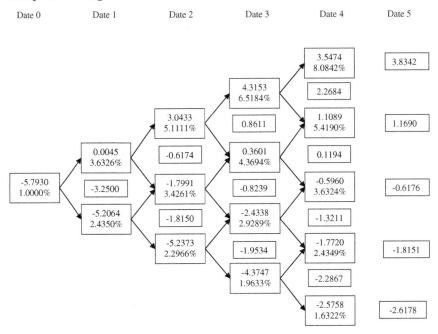

Exhibit V-7 from the perspective of the fixed-rate payer. The projected settlement payments and values are positive at the top of the tree and negative at the bottom. Using backward induction, the Date-0 VND for the swap is again −5.7930.

Exhibit V-8 introduces the assumptions about the credit risk of the two counterparties to the swap and calculates the CVA/DVA for each. The corporate payer of the fixed rate has an assumed conditional default probability of 2.25% and a recovery rate of 40% for each year. The commercial bank receiver has a conditional default probability of 0.50% and a recovery rate of 10%. The loss severities are 60% and 90%, respectively. These assumptions pertain to Date 0; the relative credit risks might have been different when the swap was initiated. Presumably, the CVA and DVA estimates calculated at that time were factored into the initial pricing of the swap, whereby "pricing" means determining the fixed rate needed to make the fair value zero. That fixed rate was 4.25%.

Exhibit V-8: CVA and DVA Calculations on the 4.25%, 5-Year, Interest Rate Swap

Credit Risk of the Fixed-Rate Payer

Credit Risk Parameters: 2.25% Conditional Probability of Default, 40% Recovery Rate

Date	Expected Exposure	LGD	POD	Discount Factor	CVA/DVA
1	5.8510	3.5106	2.25000%	0.990099	0.0782
2	3.2707	1.9624	2.19938%	0.960978	0.0415
3	2.2244	1.3346	2.14989%	0.928023	0.0266
4	1.6467	0.9880	2.10152%	0.894344	0.0186
5	0.8490	0.5094	2.05423%	0.860968	0.0090
			10.75501%		0.1739

Credit Risk of the Fixed-Rate Receiver

Credit Risk Parameters: 0.50% Conditional Probability of Default, 10% Recovery Rate

Date	Expected Exposure	LGD	POD	Discount Factor	CVA/DVA
1	0.0000	0.0000	0.50000%	0.990099	0.0000
2	0.6065	0.5458	0.49750%	0.960978	0.0026
3	0.7891	0.7102	0.49501%	0.928023	0.0033
4	0.9392	0.8453	0.49254%	0.894344	0.0037
5	0.5319	0.4787	0.49007%	0.860968	0.0020
			2.47512%		0.0116

The CVA/DVA on Date 0 for the corporate fixed-rate payer is 0.1739, considerably higher than 0.0116 for the bank fixed-rate receiver. That difference is driven by the relative expected exposures to loss following default by the counterparty. Exhibit V-9 displays the expected exposure facing the bank if the corporate payer defaults. These are the calculations for Date 3, using the swap values and settlement payments from Exhibit V-7 with the signs reserved because the exposure is to the fixed-rate receiver:

At 6.5184%   Max $[0, -4.3153 - 0.8611] = 0$
At 4.3694%   Max $[0, -0.3601 + (-0.8611 + 0.8239)/2] = 0$
At 2.9289%   Max $[0, 2.4338 + (0.8239 + 1.9534)/2] = 3.8224$
At 1.9633%   Max $[0, 4.3747 + 1.9534] = 6.3281$

The expected exposure for Date 3 is 2.2244: $(0.125*0) + (0.375*0) + (0.375*3.8224) + (0.125*6.3281) = 2.2244$. As a seasoned, off-market interest rate swap, the VND has migrated from zero at inception to be negative to the corporation and positive to the commercial bank. Because swap market rates have come down, the bank is now more

Exhibit V-9: Expected Exposure to the Fixed-Rate Receiver if the Payer Defaults

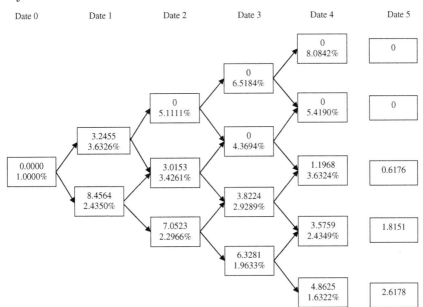

exposed to loss due to default by its corporate counterparty than the corporation is exposed to default by the bank.

The expected exposures facing the corporation if its bank counterparty defaults are shown in Exhibit V-10. These are the calculations for Date 2, using the swap values and settlement payments from Exhibit V-7:

At 5.1111% Max $[0, 3.0433 - 0.6174] = 2.4259$
At 3.4261% Max $[0, -1.7991 + (-0.6174 - 1.8150)/2] = 0$
At 2.2966% Max $[0, -5.2373 - 1.8150] = 0$

The expected exposure for Date 2 is 0.6065 in Exhibit V-8:$(0.25 * 2.4259) + (0.50 * 0) + (0.25 * 0) = 0.6065$.

Equation (1) is used to get the fair value of the swap to the two counterparties:

To the fixed-rate receiver:

$$\text{Value}^{\text{SWAP}} = +5.7930 - 0.1739 + 0.0116 = +5.6307$$

Exhibit V-10: Expected Exposure to the Fixed-Rate Payer if the Receiver Defaults

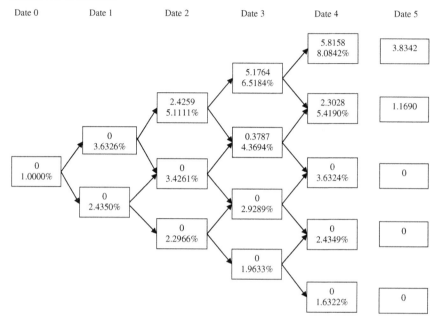

To the fixed-rate payer:

$$\text{Value}^{\text{SWAP}} = -5.7930 - 0.0116 + 0.1739 = -5.6307$$

To the commercial bank, the value of the swap is the VND (+5.7930) from its perspective, minus the CVA of the corporate counterparty (0.1739), plus its own DVA (0.0116). To the corporation, the payer swap value is the VND (−5.7930), minus of CVA of the bank counterparty (0.0116), plus its own DVA (0.1739). These fair values, +5.6307 and −5.6307, reflect the unsecured status of the derivative and would be reported on the balance sheets of the commercial bank and the corporation, probably aggregated with any other interest rate swaps.

Suppose that on Date 0 there is a significant change in the regulatory environment requiring that all derivatives be fully collateralized or centrally cleared. Assume that this action effectively makes the recovery rates approach 100%, so that the CVA and DVA for both counterparties become zero. Then the swap values reflect only the VND. It is perhaps a surprising result that credit risk mitigation that allows the commercial bank to report a larger (and safer) financial asset also means that the corporation now reports a larger liability even though that obligation represents less risk to its creditor. Moreover, the corporation needs to post collateral in the amount of 5.7930, not 5.6307, as that larger amount becomes the fair value of the swap to the bank counterparty.

V.4: Valuing the 4.25% Fixed-Rate Interest Rate Swap as a Combination of Bonds

The valuation of an interest rate swap as a long/short combination of bonds, one bond having a fixed coupon rate and the other a rate that varies from period to period, is a standard topic in derivatives and fixed-income textbooks. In practice, this interpretation is also used to infer the risk statistics for the swap, for instance, its effective duration and basis-point-value. To the fixed-rate payer, the swap is an implicit long position in a (low-duration) floating-rate note and a short position in a (higher-duration) fixed-rate bond. The duration of the swap is the difference in the durations of the two implicit bonds. Therefore, the duration of a pay-fixed swap is negative, meaning that value of the swap goes up when market rates go up. Similarly, the swap has positive duration to the receiver because it is a combination of a high-duration asset and a low-duration liability. To complete the analogy, the par values on the implicit bonds match the notional principal on the swap and the interest payment dates match the timing of the net settlements.

To assess the valuations produced by the combination-of-bonds analogy, suppose that instead of entering the 4.25% fixed-rate swap in the previous example, the corporation and commercial bank actually exchanged bond holdings several years ago. The corporation issued and sold to the commercial bank a 4.25%, annual payment bond. At the same time, the commercial bank issued and sold to the corporation a floating-rate note paying the 1-year benchmark rate flat in arrears. Both bonds have a par value of 100 and currently have five years remaining until maturity. The credit risk of the two bond issuers follows the assumptions used to value the interest rate swap in Section V.3.

Exhibit V-11 displays the valuation of the 4.25%, 5-year fixed rate bond issued by the corporation. The VND is 105.7930 and the CVA is 6.3116, based on an assumed conditional probability of default of 2.25% and a recovery rate of 40% for each year. That gives a fair

Exhibit V-11: Valuation of the Seasoned, 4.25%, 5-Year, Annual Coupon Payment Corporate Bond

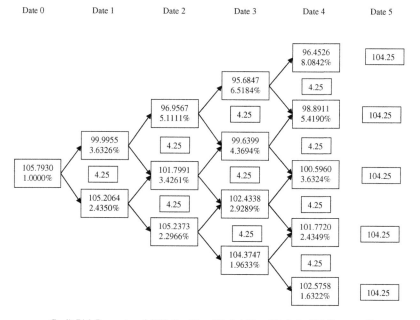

Credit Risk Parameters: 2.25% Conditional Probability of Default, 40% Recovery Rate

Date	Expected Exposure	LGD	POD	Discount Factor	CVA
1	106.8510	64.1106	2.25000%	0.990099	1.4282
2	105.6981	63.4188	2.19938%	0.960978	1.3404
3	105.0350	63.0210	2.14989%	0.928023	1.2574
4	104.5785	62.7471	2.10152%	0.894344	1.1793
5	104.2500	62.5500	2.05423%	0.860968	1.1063
			10.75501%		6.3116

Fair Value = 105.7930 − 6.3116 = 99.4815 (99.48146904)

Exhibit V-12: Valuation of a 5-Year, Seasoned Floating-Rate Bond Paying the 1-Year Rate Flat

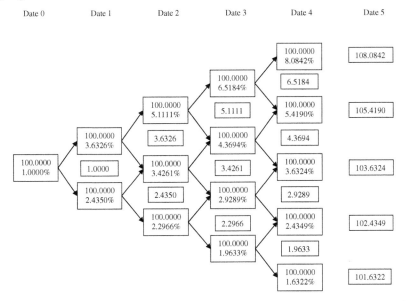

Credit Risk Parameters: 0.50% Conditional Probability of Default, 10% Recovery Rate

Date	Expected Exposure	LGD	POD	Discount Factor	CVA
1	101.0000	90.9000	0.50000%	0.990099	0.4500
2	103.0338	92.7304	0.49750%	0.960978	0.4433
3	103.5650	93.2085	0.49501%	0.928023	0.4282
4	103.7971	93.4174	0.49254%	0.894344	0.4115
5	103.9329	93.5396	0.49007%	0.860968	0.3947
			2.47512%		2.1277

Fair Value = 100.0000 − 2.1277 = 97.8723   (97.87230347)

value of 99.4815. The VND of the floating-rate note issued by the commercial bank, shown in Exhibit V-12, is 100.0000, as would be expected for a straight floater paying the reference rate flat. Each yearend interest payment corresponds to the 1-year rate observed at the beginning of the year and the floater is valued at par at each node in the tree. The CVA is 2.1277 given the 0.50% conditional default probability and 10% recovery rate for the bank. The fair value for the floater is 97.8723.

These results are summarized in the following table:

	VND	CVA	Fair Value
4.25% Fixed-Rate Bond	105.7930	6.3116	99.4815
Floating-Rate Note	100.0000	2.1277	97.8723
Combination of Bonds	5.7930		1.6092

In Section V.3, the swap is shown to have a VND of 5.7930 and a fair value of 5.6307 — a positive amount to the fixed-rate receiver and negative to the payer. Here, the combination-of-bonds approach produces the *same* VND of 5.7930 but a fair value of only 1.6092 after including credit risk present in the two bonds. The reason for the discrepancy is that the credit risk on an interest rate swap is significantly less than on a bond. The difference shows up in the expected exposures in Exhibits V-8, V-11, and V-12, in particular, because the principal is only notional on the swap whereas it is a significant element in potential loss due to default by the bond issuer.

This example illustrates a significant point about interest rate swap valuation: *The long/short combination-of-bonds approach is accurate only on risk-free derivatives and should be used with caution on swaps that are not collateralized or centrally cleared.* This is important in financial markets that have thinly traded derivatives. In that case, valuing an interest rate swap by comparing the observed market prices on risky fixed-rate and floating-rate bonds issued by the swap counterparties could produce a misleading result.

V.5: Valuing the 4.25% Fixed-Rate Interest Rate Swap as a Cap-Floor Combination

Another interpretation for an interest rate swap is a long/short combination of an interest rate cap and an interest rate floor, whereby the strike rate on each is the same as the fixed rate on the swap.[5] In addition, the notional principals and settlement dates are assumed to match. This analogy offers some insight into swap applications and poses another method to obtain a fair value for a swap. In essence, *cap-floor-swap parity* is the multi-period version of *put-call-forward parity* that is commonly used to teach (and value) options.

The relationship between the swap and a cap-floor combination can be described as follows:

$+$ Interest Rate Swap

$$= + \text{Interest Rate Cap} - \text{Interest Rate Floor} \qquad (2)$$

$-$ Interest Rate Swap

$$= - \text{Interest Rate Cap} + \text{Interest Rate Floor} \qquad (3)$$

In equation (2), the long position in the swap (the fixed-rate payer, the "buyer" of the reference rate) is equivalent to buying a cap and writing a floor. All of the net settlement cash inflows on the payer swap when the reference rate exceeds the fixed rate are the same as the inflows from owning a comparable rate cap — and all of the net settlement cash outflows when the reference rate is less than the fixed rate are the same as the outflows from having written a rate floor. In equation (3), the short position in the swap (the fixed-rate receiver, the "seller" of the reference rate) is equivalent to writing the cap and buying the floor.

This parity condition suggests that the benefits to the fixed-rate payer on the swap when rates rise are the same as on buying a rate cap. If the trade is purely speculative, the view is that rates on average will be in the top part of the binomial tree. Said differently, the reference rate is expected to track a path on average above the implied forward curve that is used to build the tree. If the trade is intended to hedge some risk exposure, the gains on the pay-fixed swap are the same as the gains on the cap, which offset the loss on the underlying position. Therefore, the key decision in choosing to hedge (or speculate) with a pay-fixed swap or with an interest rate cap is *when* and *how much* to pay for those potential benefits. If the swap is chosen, those payments are *time-deferred* and *rate-contingent*. If the cap is chosen, the payment (the option premium) is a known amount paid upfront.

Likewise, the benefits to the fixed-rate receiver on the swap are the same as those from buying the rate floor. If the swap is chosen, the cost of the "embedded floor" that is purchased is covered by the "embedded cap" that is written. The payments made on the embedded cap depend on when and to what extent future reference rates exceed the fixed rate. If instead a standalone interest rate floor is chosen to speculate that rates will be on average low, or to hedge the risk of low rates, the full payment for the transaction is made up-front on Date 0.

Suppose for this example that instead of the corporation and commercial bank entering a 4.25% fixed-rate swap a few years ago, they exchanged multi-year option contracts. The corporation wrote and sold to the bank an interest rate floor agreement having a strike rate of 4.25%. The bank in turn wrote and sold to the corporation an interest rate cap for the same strike rate of 4.25%. The interest rate cap and floor agreements, which settle in arrears based on the 1-year benchmark rate that is observed at the beginning of the year, have five years remaining until expiration and notional principals that match the interest rate swap.

If the comparable swap was an at-market transaction at inception, its initial value was zero. Therefore, the fair values of the interest rate cap and floor were also equal, independent of the volatility assumption used to value the multi-year options. Now, on Date 0, the floor should have greater value than the cap because market rates are lower. The comparable pay-fixed swap is a liability to the corporation, so the value of its asset (the cap) is less than the value of its liability (the floor) regardless of whether volatility has gone up or down since inception. Likewise, the receive-fixed swap is an asset to the bank on Date 0 and the implicit floor it owns is worth more than the implicit cap it has written.

Exhibits V-13 and V-14 show the calculations for the 4.25% interest rate cap and floor for the VND and the fair value after including credit risk. For example, on Date 3 the value of the cap

Exhibit V-13: Valuation of a 5-Year, 4.25%, Interest Rate Cap on the 1-Year Rate

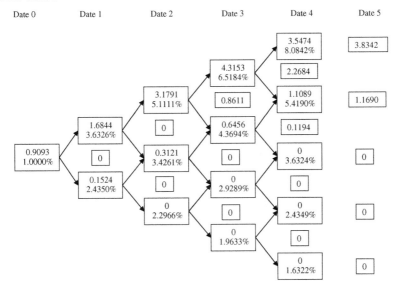

Credit Risk Parameters: 0.50% Conditional Probability of Default, 10% Recovery Rate

Date	Expected Exposure	LGD	POD	Discount Factor	CVA
1	0.9184	0.8265	0.50000%	0.990099	0.0041
2	0.9508	0.8557	0.49750%	0.960978	0.0041
3	0.9968	0.8971	0.49501%	0.928023	0.0041
4	0.8273	0.7445	0.49254%	0.894344	0.0033
5	0.5319	0.4787	0.49007%	0.860968	0.0020
			2.47512%		0.0176

Fair Value = 0.9093 – 0.0176 = 0.8917   (0.89168700)

in Exhibit V-13 is 4.3153 at the node where the benchmark rate is 6.5184%:

$$\frac{2.2684 + [(0.50 * 3.5474) + (0.050 * 1.1089]}{1.065184} = 4.3153$$

The first term in the numerator is the payment received from the cap writer at the end of the year on Date 4: $(0.065184 - 0.0425) * 100 = 2.2684$. The second term is the expected value of the cap given the 50–50 odds of the rate rising or falling at that node. The cap value

Exhibit V-14: Valuation of a 5-Year, 4.25%, Interest Rate Floor on the 1-Year Rate

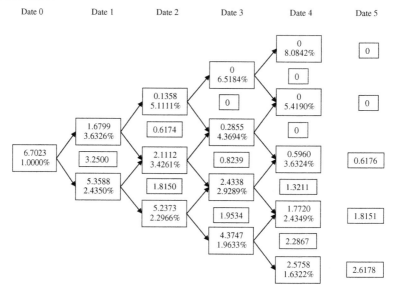

Credit Risk Parameters: 2.25% Conditional Probability of Default, 40% Recovery Rate

Date	Expected Exposure	LGD	POD	Discount Factor	CVA
1	6.7693	4.0616	2.25000%	0.990099	0.0905
2	3.6151	2.1691	2.19938%	0.960978	0.0458
3	2.4669	1.4801	2.14989%	0.928023	0.0295
4	1.6087	0.9652	2.10152%	0.894344	0.0181
5	0.8490	0.5094	2.05423%	0.860968	0.0090
			10.75501%		0.1930

Fair Value = 6.7023 − 0.1930 = 6.5093   (6.50930506)

on Date 3 at that node is the present value of the scheduled payment and the expected value.

In Exhibit V-13, the VND for the 4.25% interest rate cap written by the commercial bank is 0.9093 and its fair value is 0.8917 after subtracting the CVA of 0.0176, which is based on the assumed credit risk parameters of the commercial bank (0.50% conditional default probability and 10% recovery). The VND in Exhibit V-14 for the 4.25% floor written by the corporation is 6.7023 and the fair value is 6.5093, after subtracting the CVA of 0.1930. That credit risk is based on the assumed conditional probability of default by the corporation of 2.25% and recovery rate of 40% for each year. As expected, the value of the interest rate floor is considerably higher than the cap. These results are summarized in the following table:

	VND	CVA	Fair Value
4.25% Interest Rate Cap	0.9093	0.0176	0.8917
4.25% Interest Rate Floor	6.7023	0.1930	6.5093
Cap-Floor Combination	−5.7930		−5.6176

The interest rate cap-floor combination has the *same* value as the pay-fixed swap assuming no default; both have a VND of −5.7930. However, difference in the fair values of the options after subtracting the CVA is a bit different. Here it is −5.6176 whereas in Section V.3 the fair value of the pay-fixed swap is calculated to be −5.6307. Notice that the result for the cap-floor combination is much closer to the fair value of the swap than the long-short combination of bonds. In Section V.4, the difference in the fair values of the floating-rate note and fixed-rate bond is −1.6092, significantly misrepresenting the fair value of the swap.

This example demonstrates that the credit risk on an interest rate swap is almost the same as on the cap-floor combination but quite different than the combination of bonds. This is because the calculation of the expected exposure on a bond includes the potential loss of principal, whereas on swaps, caps, and floors the principal is merely notional. Still, the cap-floor option combination produces an accurate fair value only on a risk-free interest rate swap, for instance, one that is fully collateralized or centrally cleared.

V.6: Effective Duration and Convexity of an Interest Rate Swap

The effective duration and convexity risk statistics can be estimated for an interest rate swap using the binomial trees. Consider the 5-year, annual-settlement-in-arrears, non-collateralized, 4.25%, fixed-rate swap against the 1-year benchmark yield discussed in Sections V.3, V.4, and V.5. Using the results in Exhibits V-7 and V-8, this off-market swap is shown to have a fair value of +5.6307 to the fixed-rate receiver and −5.6307 to the fixed-rate payer. The credit risk adjustments to the VND are based on an assumed default probability of 0.50% and a recovery rate of 10% on the part of the fixed-rate receiver (a commercial bank) and a default probability of 2.25% and a recovery rate of 40% for the payer (a corporation).

Equations (11) and (12) from Chapter II need to be amended slightly to get the effective duration and convexity of an interest rate swap. These are the new versions:

$$\text{Effective Duration} = \frac{(MV_-) - (MV_+)}{2 * \Delta\text{Curve} * (|MV_0|)} \tag{4}$$

$$\text{Effective Convexity} = \frac{(MV_-) + (MV_+) - [2 * (MV_0)]}{(\Delta\text{Curve})^2 * (|MV_0|)} \tag{5}$$

To deal with the possibility of negative initial market values for the swap, the denominator now uses the *absolute value* of MV_0. This is not needed with fixed-rate and floating-rate bonds, nor with interest rate caps and floors that always have a non-negative value to the asset-holder.

To get MV_- and MV_+, the benchmark par curve is raised and lowered by 5 basis points and the new binomial trees are calibrated, as described in Chapter II. The new trees are shown previously in Exhibits II-9 and II-11. Exhibit V-15-A reports that the interest rate swap has an effective duration of −82.5903 and an effective convexity of −462.4964 from the perspective of the fixed-rate payer, based on the fair values following the 5-basis-point bumps to the benchmark bond par curve. To the fixed-rate receiver, these risk statistics are +82.5903 and +462.4964, respectively. The payer swap has negative duration and the receiver swap positive duration as is expected; however, these numbers must be interpreted with caution. Suppose that instead of this derivative, the 5-year, 2.99378% fixed-rate swap that is discussed in Section V.2 is analyzed. That swap has a fair value of +0.0000 to the fixed-rate receiver. Its effective duration and convexity statistics based on equations (4) and (5) would approach

Exhibit V-15: Effective Duration, Effective Convexity, and BPV Calculations

A. 5-Year, 4.25% Pay-Fixed Interest Rate Swap on the 1-Year Rate

$$
\begin{array}{ll}
& \text{Fair Value} \\
MV_0 & -5.63074603 \\
MV_+ & -5.39854914 \\
MV_- & -5.86359397
\end{array}
$$

Credit Risk Parameters: 2.25% Default Probability and 40% Recovery Rate for the Fixed-Rate Payer and 0.50% Default Probability and 10% Recovery Rate for the Fixed-Rate Receiver

$$\text{Effective Duration} = \frac{(-5.86359397) - (-5.39854914)}{2 * 0.0005 * (|-5.63074603|)} = -82.5903$$

$$\text{Effective Convexity} = \frac{(-5.86359397) + (-5.39854914) - (2 * -5.63074603)}{(0.0005)^2 * (|-5.63074603|)}$$

$$= -462.4964$$

Basis Point Value $= -82.5903 * |-5.63074603| * 0.0001 = -0.0465045$

B. 5-Year, 4.25% Fixed-Rate Corporate Bond

$$
\begin{array}{ll}
& \text{Fair Value} \\
MV_0 \text{ (Exhibit V-11)} & 99.48146904 \\
MV_+ & 99.25673095 \\
MV_- & 99.70683936
\end{array}
$$

Credit Risk Parameters: 2.25% Default Probability, 40% Recovery Rate

$$\text{Effective Duration} = \frac{(99.70683936) - (99.25673095)}{2 * 0.0005 * (99.48146904)} = 4.5245$$

$$\text{Effective Convexity} = \frac{(99.70683936) + (99.25673095) - (2 * 99.48146904)}{(0.0005)^2 * (99.48146904)}$$

$$= 25.4198$$

Basis Point Value $= 4.5245 * 99.48146904 * 0.0001 = 0.0450104$

C. 5-Year, Floating-Rate Corporate Bond Paying the 1-Year Rate Flat

$$
\begin{array}{ll}
& \text{Fair Value} \\
MV_0 \text{ (Exhibit V-12)} & 97.87230347 \\
MV_+ & 97.87431519 \\
MV_- & 97.87028766
\end{array}
$$

Exhibit V-15: (*Continued*)

Credit Risk Parameters: 0.50% Default Probability, 10% Recovery Rate

$$\text{Effective Duration} = \frac{(97.87028766) - (97.87431519)}{2 * 0.0005 * (97.87230347)} = -0.0412$$

$$\text{Effective Convexity} = \frac{(97.87028766) + (97.87431519) - (2 * 99.48146904)}{(0.0005)^2 * (97.87230347)}$$

$$= -0.1635$$

$$\text{Basis Point Value} = -0.0412 * 97.87230347 * 0.0001 = -0.0004032$$

D. 5-Year, 4.25% Interest Rate Cap on the 1-Year Rate

	Fair Value
MV_0 (Exhibit V-13)	0.89168700
MV_+	0.95423085
MV_-	0.82885399

Credit Risk Parameters: 0.50% Default Probability, 10% Recovery Rate

$$\text{Effective Duration} = \frac{(0.82885399) - (0.95423085)}{2 * 0.0005 * (0.89168700)} = -140.6064$$

$$\text{Effective Convexity} = \frac{(0.82885399) + (0.95423085) - (2 * 0.89168700)}{(0.0005)^2 * (0.89168700)}$$

$$= -1,297.1368$$

$$\text{Basis Point Value} = -140.6064 * 0.89168700 * 0.0001 = -0.0125377$$

E. 5-Year, 4.25% Interest Rate Floor on the 1-Year Rate

	Fair Value
MV_0 (Exhibit V-14)	6.50930506
MV_+	6.33914342
MV_-	6.67983159

Credit Risk Parameters: 2.25% Default Probability, 40% Recovery Rate

$$\text{Effective Duration} = \frac{(6.67983159) - (6.33914342)}{2 * 0.0005 * (6.50930506)} = 52.3386$$

$$\text{Effective Convexity} = \frac{(6.67983159) + (6.33914342) - (2 * 6.50930506)}{(0.0005)^2 * (6.50930506)}$$

$$= 224.2267$$

$$\text{Basis Point Value} = 52.3386 * 6.50930506 * 0.0001 = 0.0340688$$

infinity because the fair value (MV_0 in the denominator) rounds to zero.

The problem is that effective duration (and the effective convexity adjustment) measures a *percentage price change*. That produces a useful risk measure for fixed-rate bonds. However, for interest rate derivatives often a better measure is the *basis-point-value*, which indicates the change in the market value in currency units given a 1-basis-point change in the interest rate level. The basis-point-value (BPV) is calculated as:

$$BPV = \text{Effective Duration} * |\text{Market Value}| * 0.0001 \qquad (6)$$

Note that multiplying the effective duration by (the absolute value of) the market value cancels out the $|MV_0|$ term in the denominator of equation (4), eliminating the "blowing up" problem for a derivative having a market value close or equal to zero. Related statistics are called the PV01, the present value of a 1-basis-point change (the 01) and the DV01, the dollar value of the 01 shift. The effective duration times the market value is called the *money duration* (or dollar duration). The effective convexity times the market value is the *money convexity* (or dollar convexity).

In Exhibit V-15-A, the BPV for the payer swap is −0.0465045. This is per 100 in notional principal. If the notional principal on the swap is $25 million and the benchmark bond par curve jumps up by 10 basis points, the estimated *increase* in fair value to the fixed-rate payer is $116,261 $[= -(\$25,000,000/100 * -0.0465045 * 10)]$. The estimated decrease in fair value to the fixed-rate receiver is also $116,261. Note that the same estimate can be obtained using the effective duration of −82.5903 and the fair value of the swap, scaled for the notional principal:

$$-82.5903 * [(\$25,000,000/100) * -5.63074603] * 0.0010 = \$116,261$$

The calculations are the same but implementation with the BPV typically is easier. Note that the estimate could be improved by adding in the convexity adjustment. The key point is that the effective duration statistic $(+/-82.5903)$ is not wrong; rather it just must be used with caution because as a percentage change it depends critically on the initial value.

The example in Section V.4 shows that a 4.25% fixed-rate interest rate swap can be interpreted as a long/short combination of a 4.25% fixed-rate note and a floating-rate note paying the 1-year benchmark rate. Exhibits V-15-B and V-15-C examine the risk statistics for the two implicit debt securities. The 5-year, 4.25% fixed-rate note has a fair value of 99.48146904 assuming a 2.25% conditional default probability and a 40% recovery rate, which match the credit risk parameters for the corporate fixed-rate payer on the swap. The risk statistics are an effective duration of 4.5245, an effective convexity of 25.4198, and a BPV of 0.0450104.

The 5-year, floating-rate note has fair value of 97.87230347 given the default probability of 0.50% and the recovery rate of 10% for each year, matching those for the commercial bank fixed-rate receiver on the swap. Its effective duration is −0.0412, its effective convexity is −0.1635, and its BPV is −0.0004032. Those negative numbers arise because the implicit floater is priced at a discount below par value.

Using the combination-of-bonds approach, the effective duration and convexity statistics for the interest rate swap from the perspective of the corporate fixed-rate payer are −4.5657 [=−0.0412−4.5245] and −25.5833 [=(−0.1635 − 25.4198], respectively. These are the risk statistics for the FRN minus those for the fixed-rate note. Note that these are really just approximations for the percentage price change because the fair values on the implicit bonds are not the same. In any case, they are significantly different than the effective duration and convexity reported in Exhibit V-15-A where effective duration is −82.5903 and the convexity is −462.4964. The differences are significant because the bond prices are close to par value whereas the swap value is much closer to zero. On a percentage basis, the changes in value are substantially different when the benchmark par curve is bumped up and down.

The BPVs are much closer between the bond combination and the swap. The BPV for the FRN/fixed-rate bond combination is −0.0454136(= −0.0004032 − 0.0450104) while the BPV for the swap is −0.0465045. The small difference arises because of the credit risk adjustments and the differences between the expected exposure to default loss on the bonds and the swap, in particular, because the principal is merely notional on the derivative. If the credit risk on the swap approaches zero, for instance if the deal is fully collateralized or centrally cleared, the BPVs based on the VND numbers are identical for the swap and the combination of bonds.

In practice, the duration of a newly issued, at-market, interest rate swap is usually reported using the combination-of-bonds approach and not as an effective duration using equation (4). That is because an at-market swap has a fair value of zero at inception and any change in value on a percentage basis is infinite. The idea is that this swap has changes in dollar value that are very similar to the implicit fixed-rate bond (as indicated by the similar BPVs) when rates change, and therefore should have a similar price sensitivity statistic. Note that the implicit bonds are both assumed to be priced at par, so subtracting the percentage price changes is not a problem. Some applications for interest rate swaps entail adjusting the average duration of a fixed-income bond portfolio to some new target duration. The effective duration of the swap as it relates to bonds is used to determine the size of the "derivatives overlay" needed to move the portfolio duration to the target.[6]

The other interpretation for an interest rate swap shown in this exposition is a cap-floor combination. Exhibits V-15-D and V-15-E report the calculations for the two five-year option contracts. The 4.25% cap has a fair value of 0.89168700 (per 100 of notional principal) based on the same credit risk parameters as the commercial bank that is the fixed-rate receiver on the swap. This cap has an effective duration of −140.6064 and an effective convexity of −1,297.1368. The high percentage price changes result from the low option value on Date 0. The BPV for the cap is −0.0125377 per 100 in notional principal. The 4.25% interest rate floor has a fair value of 6.50930506 based on an assumed default probability of 2.25% and a recovery rate of 40% for each year to match the parameters for the corporate fixed-rate payer on the swap. The effective duration is 52.3386, the effective convexity is 224.2267, and the BPV is 0.0340688.

The signs for the effective durations of the cap and floor make sense. The cap has negative duration because it gains value when benchmark bond rates go up. While negative duration is rare on debt securities (and negative convexity limited mostly to callable bonds), it is common with interest rate derivatives — both payer swaps and interest rate caps have negative effective durations. The positive duration on the interest rate floor agreement indicates that it gains value when benchmark rates go down, just like a receiver swap.

The example in Section V.5 explains that a payer swap has the same promised cash flows as owning an interest rate cap that is financed by writing a floor. The strike rates are the same as the fixed rate on the swap. This combination suggests that the effective duration for the swap is $-192.9450(= -140.6064 - 52.3386)$ and the effective convexity is $-1,521.3635(= -1,297.1368 - 224.2267)$. The numbers, however, reveal the folly of adding and subtracting percentage price changes without adjusting for the differences in the initial prices.

On the other hand, the BPV for the cap-floor combination is reasonable because the price is included in the risk statistic. The BPV is $-0.0466065(= -0.0125377 - 0.0340688)$. This is very close to the BPV for the swap of -0.0465045 reported in Exhibit V-15-A. Moreover, it is much closer than the BPV for the combination of bonds, which is -0.0454136. As in Section V.4, the difference in credit risk drives these outcomes. A long/short combination of an interest rate cap and a floor is more similar to an interest rate swap in terms of expected exposure to default loss than a combination of bonds.

In sum, the most relevant risk statistic for an interest rate swap typically is its BPV (or PV01 or DV01). Its effective duration can be inferred from the combination-of-bonds approach, but for risk measurement calculations the more useful statistic is the estimated change in fair value per basis point. This could be adjusted for convexity, although that is not commonly done in practice. The BPV can be calculated directly using the binomial forward rate trees. As demonstrated, it can be estimated using the BPVs of the implicit fixed-rate bond and floating-rate note. However, the estimation suffers from the difference in credit risk on the swap and the bonds. A better estimation results from using the BPVs of the implicit interest rate cap and floor agreements because their credit risks are more similar to that of a swap.

V.7: Study Questions

(A) A commercial bank has on its books a 5-year, 3.25%, annual-net-settlement-in-arrears, receive-fixed interest rate swap with a corporate counterparty referencing the 1-year benchmark rate. The notional principal is $50,000,000. The assumed credit risk parameters for the corporation paying the fixed rate are a conditional default probability of 1.75% and a recovery rate of 40% for each year. The bank has a conditional probability of default of 0.50% and a recovery rate of 10% if default occurs. Calculate the fair value of the interest rate swap to the bank as a standalone contract.

(B) The commercial bank also has a 4-year, 4.00% pay-fixed swap on its books with the same corporation. This swap has a notional principal of $25,000,000. Calculate the fair value of this swap to the bank, again as a standalone contract.

(C) Now assume that the two swaps are documented under the ISDA agreement calling for closeout netting. That means if either counterparty were to default, the two swaps would be combined to determine the net fair value. Calculate the combined fair value for the two-swaps derivatives portfolio.

V.8: Answers to the Study Questions

(A) The VND for the 3.25%, 5-year, $50 million receiver swap is +$579,305 to the bank. The CVA capturing the credit risk if the corporate payer defaults is $21,071. The DVA is $15,776. These results are shown in Exhibits V-16 and V-17 and follow the steps demonstrated in Section V.3. The expected exposures using value and payment netting for the counterparties are displayed in Exhibits V-18 and V-19. The fair value of

Exhibit V-16: Valuation of a 3.25%, 5-Year, $50 Million Notional Principal, Receive-Fixed Interest Rate Swap Assuming No Default

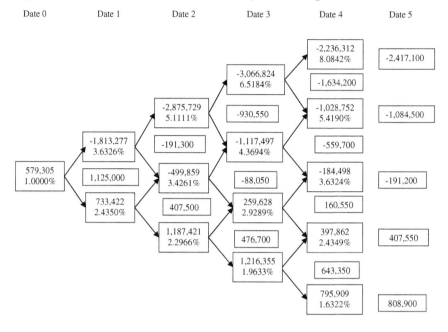

Exhibit V-17: CVA and DVA Calculations on the 3.25%, 5-Year, $50 Million Notional Principal, Interest Rate Swap

Credit Risk of the Fixed-Rate Payer

Credit Risk Parameters: 1.75% Conditional Probability of Default, 40% Recovery Rate

Date	Expected Exposure	LGD	POD	Discount Factor	CVA/DVA
1	929,211	557,527	1.75000%	0.990099	9,660
2	398,730	239,238	1.71938%	0.960978	3,953
3	381,864	229,119	1.68929%	0.928023	3,592
4	289,907	173,944	1.65972%	0.894344	2,582
5	152,444	91,466	1.63068%	0.860968	1,284
			8.44906%		21,071

Credit Risk of the Fixed-Rate Receiver

Credit Risk Parameters: 0.50% Conditional Probability of Default, 10% Recovery Rate

Date	Expected Exposure	LGD	POD	Discount Factor	CVA/DVA
1	344,113	309,702	0.50000%	0.990099	1,533
2	962,637	866,373	0.49750%	0.960978	4,142
3	1,109,721	998,749	0.49501%	0.928023	4,588
4	917,360	825,624	0.49254%	0.894344	3,637
5	493,894	444,504	0.49007%	0.860968	1,876
			2.47512%		15,776

Exhibit V-18: Expected Exposure to the 3.25% Fixed-Rate Swap if the Payer Defaults

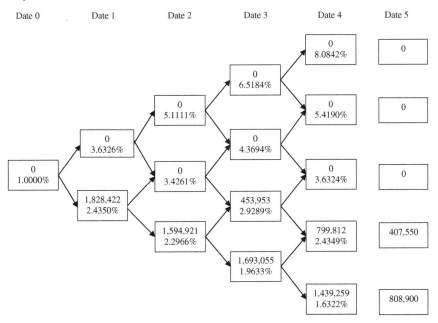

Exhibit V-19: Expected Exposure to the 3.25% Fixed-Rate Swap if the Receiver Defaults

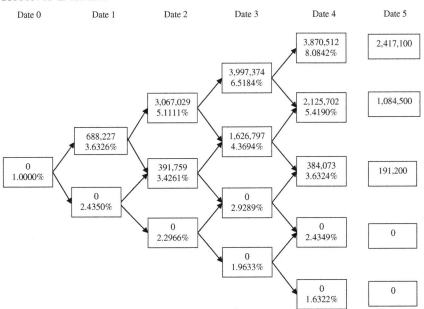

the swap to the bank on a standalone basis is +$574,009(= $579,305 − $21,071 + $15,776).

(B) The VND for the 4%, 4-year, $25 million payer swap is −$1,132,036 to the bank as calculated in Exhibit V-20. The CVA and DVA are $3,808 and $9,332, respectively, as shown in Exhibit V-21. The expected exposures using value and payment netting for corporation and the bank are in Exhibits V-22 and V-23. The fair value of the standalone swap to the bank is −$1,126,512(= −$1,132,036 − $3,808 + $9,332).

(C) To get the fair value of the two-swap portfolio assuming close-out netting, it is first necessary to redo the trees showing the expected exposures for value and payment netting. Exhibit V-24 does this for the 3.25%, $50 million, receive-fixed swap from the perspective of the bank for possible default by the corporate payer. The positive amounts are the same as in Exhibit V-18 but now the negative amounts at top of tree are shown and are not converted to zeros.

Exhibit V-20: Valuation of a 4%, 4-Year, $25 Million Notional Principal, Pay-Fixed Interest Rate Swap Assuming No Default

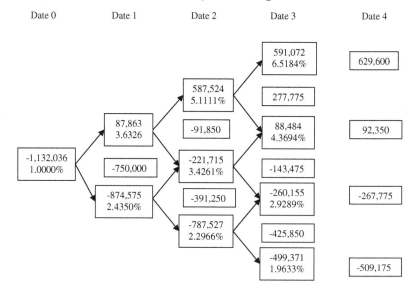

Exhibit V-21: CVA and DVA Calculations on the 4%, 4-Year, $25 Million Notional Principal, Interest Rate Swap

Credit Risk of the Fixed-Rate Payer

Credit Risk Parameters: 0.50% Conditional Probability of Default, 10% Recovery Rate

Date	Expected Exposure	LGD	POD	Discount Factor	CVA/DVA
1	1,143,356	1,029,020	0.50000%	0.990099	5,094
2	526,326	473,694	0.49750%	0.960978	2,265
3	319,959	287,963	0.49501%	0.928023	1,323
4	164,063	147,656	0.49254%	0.894344	650
			1.98505%		9,332

Credit Risk of the Fixed-Rate Receiver

Credit Risk Parameters: 1.75% Conditional Probability of Default, 40% Recovery Rate

Date	Expected Exposure	LGD	POD	Discount Factor	CVA/DVA
1	0	0	1.75000%	0.990099	0
2	123,918	74,351	1.71938%	0.960978	1,228
3	166,968	100,181	1.68929%	0.928023	1,571
4	113,331	67,999	1.65972%	0.894344	1,009
			6.81838%		3,808

Exhibit V-22: Expected Exposure to the 4% Fixed-Rate Swap if the Payer Defaults

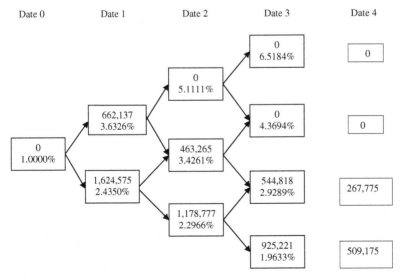

Exhibit V-23: Expected Exposure to the 4% Fixed-Rate Swap if the Receiver Defaults

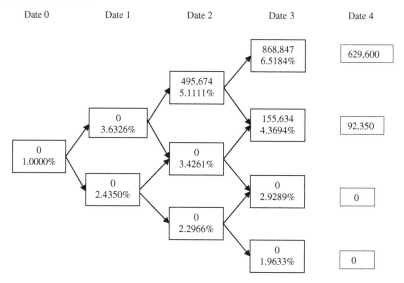

Exhibit V-24: Expected Exposures on the 5-Year, 3.25% Fixed-Rate Swap From the Bank's Perspective for Closeout Netting

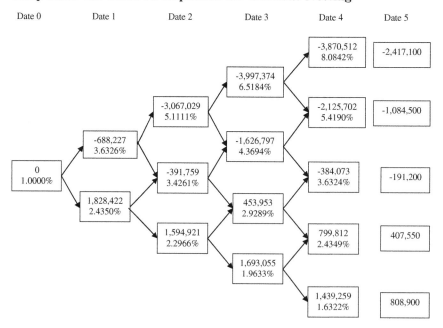

Exhibit V-25: Expected Exposures on the 4-Year, 4% Fixed-Rate Swap From the Bank's Perspective for Closeout Netting

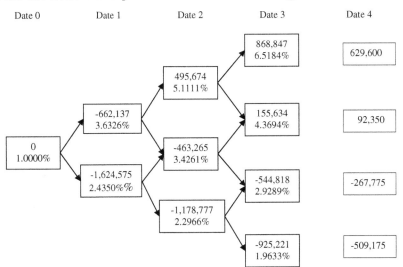

Exhibit V-25 shows the positive and negative exposures to the bank on the 4%, $25 million, pay-fixed swap. When valued on a standalone basis as in Exhibit V-23, the negative amounts are converted to zeros. Here for closeout netting, the negative amounts are retained because they can be used to offset positive exposures on the other swap.

The combined exposures on the two swaps from the perspective of the bank are presented in Exhibit V-26. At each node in the tree, the amounts from Exhibits V-24 and V-25 are added. If negative, the amount converts to zero. If positive, the net exposure is retained. These are the calculations for Date 3:

At 6.5184% Max $[0, -3{,}997{,}374 + 868{,}847] = 0$
At 4.3694% Max $[0, -1{,}626{,}797 + 155{,}634] = 0$
At 2.9289% Max $[0, 453{,}953 - 544{,}818] = 0$
At 1.9633% Max $[0, 1{,}693{,}055 - 925{,}221] = 767{,}834$

Exhibit V-27 shows the combined exposures from the perspective of the corporation. The positive and negative exposures to each individual swap are the same as Exhibits V-24 and V-25

Exhibit V-26: Expected Exposures on the Combined Swaps From the Bank's Perspective for Closeout Netting

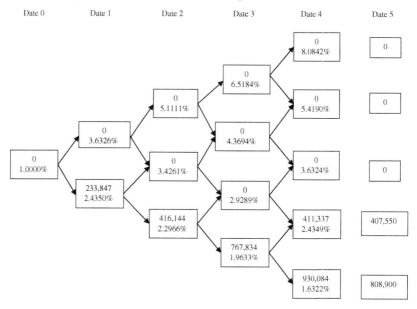

Exhibit V-27: Expected Exposures on the Combined Swaps From the Corporation's Perspective for Closeout Netting

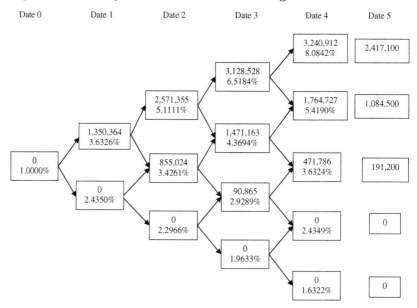

Exhibit V-28: CVA and DVA Calculations on the Combined Interest Rate Swaps

Credit Risk of the Corporate Counterparty

Credit Risk Parameters: 1.75% Conditional Probability of Default, 40% Recovery Rate

Date	Expected Exposure	LGD	POD	Discount Factor	CVA/DVA
1	116,924	70,154	1.75000%	0.990099	1,216
2	104,036	62,422	1.71938%	0.960978	1,031
3	95,979	57,588	1.68929%	0.928023	903
4	160,965	96,579	1.65972%	0.894344	1,434
5	152,444	91,466	1.63068%	0.860968	1,284
			8.44906%		5,867

Credit Risk of the Commercial Bank

Credit Risk Parameters: 0.50% Conditional Probability of Default, 10% Recovery Rate

Date	Expected Exposure	LGD	POD	Discount Factor	CVA/DVA
1	675,182	607,664	0.50000%	0.990099	3,008
2	1,070,351	963,316	0.49750%	0.960978	4,605
3	976,827	879,144	0.49501%	0.928023	4,039
4	820,658	738,593	0.49254%	0.894344	3,253
5	493,894	444,504	0.49007%	0.860968	1,876
			2.47512%		16,781

with all of the signs reversed. These are the calculations for Date 2:

At 5.1111%   Max $[0, 3,067,029 - 495,674] = 2,571,355$

At 3.4261%   Max $[0, 391,759 + 463,265] = 855,024$

At 2.2966%   Max $[0, -1,594,921 + 1,178,777] = 0$

The CVA and DVA calculations for the combined two-swap portfolio are summarized in Exhibit V-28. The CVA/DVAs for the corporation and the bank are $5,867 and $16,781, respectively.

Using the results from (A) and (B) the net fair value of the two swaps to the bank when valued on a standalone basis is $-$552,503(= \$574,009 - \$1,126,512)$. On a portfolio basis, the overall VND for the two derivatives is simply the sum of the individual VNDs: $579,305 - $1,132,036 = -$552,731$. Adjusting for the credit risk, the combined fair value to the bank is $-$541,817:

$$-\$552,731 - \$5,867 + \$16,781 = -\$541,817$$

The fair value to the corporation is +$541,817.

Endnotes

1. As stated in Endnote 2 in Chapter II, this is no doubt a high default probability for a major money-center commercial bank that is a market-maker in derivatives.
2. This is a change from previous versions of this tutorial in which the swap values and net settlement payments were not netted. Instead, any value or payment that was negative was converted to zero. The author thanks Andreas Blochlinger for the suggestion to net the values and payments first and only convert to zero those that sum to a negative amount.
3. In this exposition, there is no difference between collateralization on a bilateral OTC contract and central clearing — both are assumed to raise the recovery rate to 100% thereby reducing the loss due to counterparty default to zero. With central clearing, the periodic settlement payments go through the clearinghouse which holds collateral (i.e., margin) on the net exposure from the entire derivatives portfolio.
4. See Hull and White (2013) and Smith (2013) for further discussion of OIS discounting in interest rate swap valuation.
5. This interpretation is presented in Brown and Smith (1995), along with the usual combination-of-bonds approach. An interest rate swap also is analogized as a series of forward rate agreements on the reference rate.
6. For an example of this type of application and calculation of the requisite notional principal on the interest rate swap, see Adams and Smith (2009).

Chapter VI

Valuing an Interest Rate Swap Portfolio with CVA, DVA, and FVA

In the last few years, several large banks that are the major market makers in interest rate derivatives have included a funding valuation adjustment (FVA) in their financial statements. For example, when JP Morgan Chase first reported FVA in the 4th quarter 2013, it stated that this action was "reflecting an industry migration towards incorporating the cost or benefit of unsecured funding into valuations." At the time it recognized a one-time loss of USD 1.5 billion related to FVA. The FVA can be positive or negative. Page 4 of the January 19, 2014 release for Deutsche Bank's Corporate Banking and Securities group states: "Fourth quarter results were also affected by a EUR 110 million charge for Debt Valuation Adjustment (DVA), and a EUR 149 million charge for Credit Valuation Adjustment (CVA), which offset a gain of EUR 83 million for Funding Valuation Adjustment (FVA)."

Including funding costs and benefits in derivatives valuation is not without controversy. When FVA first appeared, John Hull and Alan White (2012, 2014) raised objections to the practice and set off a wave of papers and presentations at conferences. A strong argument against FVA is the well-established academic principle that the value of an asset does not depend on the source of funds by which it has been acquired. A Treasury bond that trades at 99 (percent of par value) is worth $990,000 for a par value of $1 million. It does not matter if the investor raised funds to buy the T-bonds by issuing equity or taking out a bank loan. Therefore, FVA is not used with the valuation of debt securities.

Interest rate derivatives are different than debt securities in that they are typically hedged in the course of doing business. The FVA is an adjustment to the value of the overall derivatives book that includes non-collateralized as well as collateralized contracts, trades with corporate customers, as well as hedges to minimize interest rate risk. To illustrate how funding costs and benefits emerge in making a market in swaps, this chapter uses a rather contained example.[1] First, the bank is assumed to enter a pay-fixed, uncollateralized swap with a corporate counterparty. The interest rate risk on the swap is then hedged in the inter-dealer market with a received-fixed, collateralized swap. The binomial tree model is used to show how the projected swap values and net settlement payments generate funding costs and benefits.

In the example, a net funding cost (FVA > 0) arises when cash collateral is posted with the dealer. That cash earns only the benchmark bond interest rate whereas the bank obtains the funds in the money market paying a spread above the benchmark. Similarly, a benefit (FVA < 0) arises when cash collateral is received. Two different methods to calculate FVA are illustrated. In this particular example, the funding benefits exceed the costs; the recognition of FVA < 0 leads to a reported gain in the financial statements. This example, albeit simplified and an abstraction from real contracts, serves to demonstrate the types of valuation models used in practice and how a negative or a positive FVA can be produced for a money-center bank that hedges uncollateralized derivatives with collateralized contracts.

VI.1: Valuing a 3.75%, 5-Year, Pay-Fixed Interest Rate Swap with CVA and DVA

Assume that two years ago a corporation and a commercial bank entered a 7-year interest rate swap contract. The bank pays a fixed rate of 3.75% and its corporate counterparty pays the 1-year benchmark rate. Net settlement is annual in arrears, meaning that the reference rate is set at the beginning of the year and settlement is at the end of the year. The corporation was motived to create a synthetic floating-rate note, whereby "synthetic" means "made with a derivative". It issued a traditional fixed-rate bond and transformed the obligation into an adjustable-rate liability by entering the receive-fixed/pay-floating exchange agreement. The idea is that this debt structure matches the corporation's revenue stream, which happens to be highly correlated to the business cycle and market interest rates.[2] The salient aspect to this swap for this chapter is that it is uncollateralized — each party bears the credit risk of the other over the lifetime of the contract.

Now, two years later, this 5-year, 3.75% fixed-rate swap contract needs to be valued by the commercial bank for financial reporting. Following the methodology presented in Chapter V, the value assuming no default (VND) is calculated using the binomial tree for 1-year benchmark bond interest rates assuming 20% volatility. Then the credit and debit risk adjustments (CVA and DVA) are added to capture counterparty credit risk. For this example, the corporation is assumed to have a conditional default probability of 1.50% and a recovery rate of 30% for each year. The commercial bank is assumed to have a default probability of 0.50% and a recovery rate of 10%.

Exhibit VI-1 shows the binomial tree for the VND from the perspective of the commercial bank paying the 3.75% fixed rate. That the VND is −3.4758 per 100 of notional principal is not surprising because benchmark bond interest rates are lower than when the swap was originated. As mentioned in Chapter V, the current fixed rate on an at-market (or par) swap having a fair value of zero would be 3.00% before factoring in counterparty credit risk. Therefore, a 3.75% payer swap is "underwater" and has a negative value. The bank is, in effect, paying an "above-market" fixed rate to the corporation in exchange for the 1-year benchmark rate. In fact, the VND can be calculated as the present value of the annuity representing the "deficiency" in the fixed rate. That annuity is 0.75 per 100 of notional principal: $(3.75\% - 3.00\%) * 100 = 0.75$. The present value of the annuity is

Exhibit VI-1: Valuation of a 3.75%, 5-Year, Pay-Fixed Interest Rate Swap Assuming No Default

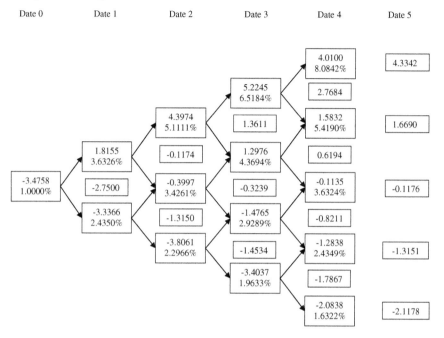

3.4758, calculated using the benchmark bond discount factors first shown in Exhibit I-3.

$$(0.75 * 0.990099) + (0.75 * 0.960978) + (0.75 * 0.928023)$$
$$+ (0.75 * 0.894344) + (0.75 * 0.860968) = 3.4758$$

This VND is negative to the commercial bank and positive to the corporate counterparty.

The CVA and DVA results are displayed in Exhibit VI-2. The CVA/DVA for the fixed-rate payer is 0.0355 per 100 of notional principal. That amount is the present value of the expected loss facing the corporate counterparty if the commercial bank defaults. In the same manner, the CVA/DVA for the receiver is 0.0419. It is the present value of expected loss following default by the corporation. To the

Exhibit VI-2: CVA and DVA Calculations on the 3.75%, 5-Year, Interest Rate Swap

Credit Risk of the Fixed-Rate Payer, the Commercial Bank

Credit Risk Parameters: 0.50% Conditional Probability of Default, 10% Recovery Rate

Date	Expected Exposure	LGD	POD	Discount Factor	CVA/DVA
1	3.5106	3.1595	0.50000%	0.990099	0.0156
2	1.8382	1.6544	0.49750%	0.960978	0.0079
3	1.4941	1.3447	0.49501%	0.928023	0.0062
4	0.9692	0.8723	0.49254%	0.894344	0.0038
5	0.5052	0.4747	0.49007%	0.860968	0.0019
			2.47512%		0.0355

Credit Risk of the Fixed-Rate Receiver, the Corporate Counterparty

Credit Risk Parameters: 1.50% Conditional Probability of Default, 30% Recovery Rate

Date	Expected Exposure	LGD	POD	Discount Factor	CVA/DVA
1	0.0000	0.0000	1.50000%	0.990099	0.0000
2	1.0700	0.7490	1.47750%	0.960978	0.0106
3	1.5043	1.0530	1.45534%	0.928023	0.0142
4	1.2429	0.8700	1.43351%	0.894344	0.0112
5	0.6881	0.4817	1.41200%	0.860968	0.0059
			7.27835%		0.0419

commercial bank, the CVA is 0.0419 and the DVA is 0.0355. The credit-risk adjusted value of the 3.75% payer swap is −3.4822.

$$\text{Value}^{\text{SWAP}} = \text{VND} - \text{CVA} + \text{DVA}$$
$$= -3.4758 - 0.0419 + 0.0355 = -3.4822$$

Exhibit VI-3 shows the expected exposures facing the commercial bank. These are calculated by netting the future net settlement payments and receipts with the swap values, as described in Chapter V. The zeros at the bottom of the tree indicate that the net swap values and payments are negative to the bank. These are the calculations for the risk exposures for Date 3:

At 6.5184%   Max $[0, 5.2245 + 1.3611] = 6.5856$
At 4.3694%   Max $[0, 1.2976 + (1.3611 - 0.3239)/2] = 1.8162$
At 2.9289%   Max $[0, -1.4765 + (-0.3239 - 1.4534)/2] = 0$
At 1.9633%   Max $[0, -3.4037 - 1.4534] = 0$

Exhibit VI-3: Expected Exposure to the Fixed-Rate Payer if the Receiver Defaults

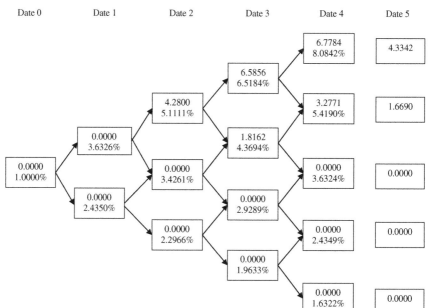

The expected exposure for Date 3 shown in the lower table in Exhibit VI-2 is 1.5043:

$$(0.125 * 6.5856) + (0.375 * 1.8162) + (0.375 * 0)$$
$$+ (0.125 * 0) = 1.5043.$$

VI.2: Valuing the Combination of the Pay-Fixed Swap and the Hedge Swap

To see how funding costs and benefits arise in the derivatives business, suppose that the commercial bank hedged its interest rate risk on the 5-year, 3.75% *pay-fixed* swap with the corporate counterparty with a 3.80% *receive-fixed* swap in the inter-dealer market. Both swaps are tied to the 1-year benchmark rate, make annual net settlement payments in arrears, and have the same notional principal. The combination of receiving the floating reference rate from the corporation and paying that same rate to the dealer eliminates exposure to

Exhibit VI-4: The 3.75% Pay-Fixed Swap with the Corporation Hedged with the 3.80% Received-Fixed Swap in the Inter-Dealer Market

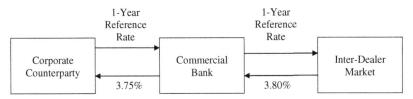

subsequent changes in the 1-year benchmark rate. This is illustrated in Exhibit VI-4. The difference in the fixed rates establishes that the profit to the bank on the hedged transaction is an annuity of five basis points per year assuming no default.

Assume that two years ago, when the 3.75% swap with the corporation and the 3.80% hedge swap were initiated, each had a tenor of seven years and an initial value of zero. In fact, the 3.75% pay-fixed rate would have been set based on the 3.80% rate on the hedge swap. A principle of OTC (over-the-counter) derivatives pricing is that the rate given a customer is a markup or markdown from the rate on the hedge product or strategy. That is, the commercial bank first identifies how the interest rate risk on the OTC derivative will be managed and then sets the rate to the customer to cover the costs and risks of hedging, as well as some target profit and compensation for un-hedged risks. The bank started with 3.80% on the receive-fixed swap in the inter-dealer market and then used a credit risk model to get the CVA and DVA. The pay-fixed rate was chosen to be 3.75% because at that rate the fair value of the swap was zero at inception.

While the interest rate risk on the OTC swap with the corporation is hedged, the credit risk is not. The bank remains at risk to changes in the CVA and DVA, in particular that the expected loss given default by the counterparty goes up. Some money-center banks in recent years have centralized CVA, thereby aggregating the credit risk exposures with counterparties arising on derivatives as well as loan contracts. Then the CVA trading desk can choose to hedge some of or all that risk using credit default swaps. The exposure

to the bank's own credit risk (to lower DVA) is much more difficult to hedge. Presumably, this risk is priced into the fixed rate on
the swap.

In Section VI.1 the fair value of the pay-fixed swap to the bank
is determined to be −3.4822 per 100 of notional principal. That liability is offset by the increased value of the receive-fixed hedge swap
as market rates have come down over the two years since inception.
Exhibit VI-5 shows that the VND for the 5-year, 3.80% receive-fixed
hedge swap with a dealer is +3.7075 per 100 of notional principal.
The key feature to this inter-dealer swap is that it is fully collateralized, presumably with cash that earns the benchmark interest
rate. Collateralization in principle renders the swap to be free of
default risk; therefore, CVA = DVA = 0 because the recovery rate is
assumed to approach 100%. This assumption about the absence of
default risk implies that some aspects of actual collateral agreements
are neglected — for instance, thresholds that indicate when collateral

**Exhibit VI-5: Valuation of a 3.80%, 5-Year, Receive-Fixed Interest
Rate Swap Assuming No Default**

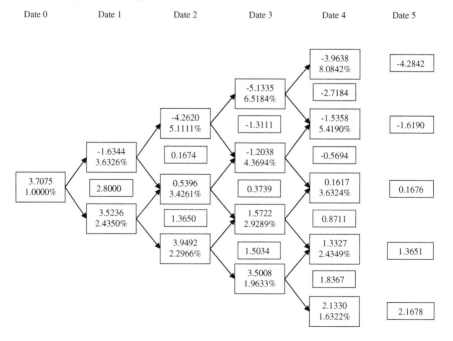

needs to be posted, minimum transfer amounts, and timeframes for the delivery of the cash.

If these two swaps comprise the commercial bank's entire derivatives portfolio, the net value is $+0.2253$ per 100 of notional principal: $-3.4822 + 3.7075 = +0.2253$. Of course, banks that are active in the OTC derivatives market have multitudes of contracts. Often the swaps provide "internal" hedges to interest rate risk, for instance, when pay-fixed swaps are offset with receive-fixed swaps with other end-users. Then the bank only uses the inter-dealer market to hedge the residual interest rate risk.

VI.3: Swap Portfolio Valuation Including FVA — First Method

Funding costs can arise from hedging an uncollateralized derivative with a comparable contract that entails posting cash collateral that earns an interest rate lower than the bank's cost of borrowed funds. The bank posts collateral on the hedge swap to cover negative values and payments. A funding benefit results from receiving cash as collateral on the hedge swap and paying a lower interest rate than the cost of funds. The FVA is the net difference between the funding cost and benefit:

$$\text{FVA} = \text{Funding Cost} - \text{Funding Benefit} \qquad (1)$$

Suppose that the commercial bank chooses to introduce the net funding costs and benefits into its valuation of the two-swaps derivatives portfolio, the 3.75% payer swap with the corporate counterparty and the 3.80% receiver swap with dealer. The funding costs and benefits arise fundamentally from the spread between the bank's 1-year cost of funds on the money market and the 1-year benchmark interest rate that applies to the cash collateral. However, there are different ways to calculate the FVA for the collateralized swap—and the financial statements of the major money-center banks that have adopted FVA in recent years do not disclose their methodology. Each of two plausible methods illustrated here and in the next section to calculate FVA rely on the same set of assumptions about the credit risk parameters for the bank.

Exhibit VI-6: First Method to Calculate the Funding Costs and Benefits

Expected Funding Costs

Date	Expected Posting of Cash Collateral	Loss Severity	POD	Discount Factor	Expected Funding Costs
1	0	90%	0.50000%	0.990099	0.0000
2	0	90%	0.49750%	0.960978	0.0000
3	1.0236	90%	0.49501%	0.928023	0.0042
4	1.4327	90%	0.49254%	0.894344	0.0057
5	1.2126	90%	0.49007%	0.860968	0.0046
					0.0145

Expected Funding Benefits

Date	Expected Receipt of Cash Collateral	Loss Severity	POD	Discount Factor	Expected Funding Benefit
1	3.7075	90%	0.50000%	0.990099	0.0165
2	3.7446	90%	0.49750%	0.960978	0.0161
3	1.9815	90%	0.49501%	0.928023	0.0082
4	1.5671	90%	0.49254%	0.894344	0.0062
5	1.0370	90%	0.49007%	0.860968	0.0039
					0.0510

FVA = Funding Costs – Funding Benefits = 0.0145 – 0.0510 = –0.0365

Note: The columns for the expected posting and receipt of cash collateral refer to the previous date. For example, the bank expects to receive 1.0370 in cash collateral on Date 4. That generates an expected funding benefit on Date 5. The present value of that benefit is of 0.0039.

Exhibit VI-6 shows the tables for the first method to calculate the FVA on the 3.80% hedge swap. These tables are similar to those used to get the CVA and DVA on an uncollateralized swap. Some arbitrary assumptions need to be made in this simple model. Cash collateral is posted once a year to cover the net settlement payment that is owed to the dealer that is the counterparty to the hedge swap and to cover a negative value to the contact on that date. The bank receives interest at the end of the year on the cash it has transferred to the dealer. Importantly, the interest rate is the 1-year benchmark rate. Similarly, cash is received from dealer when the net settlement payment is owed to the bank and to cover a positive swap value on that date. The bank then pays the dealer interest at the end of the year based on the benchmark rate. The expected amounts of collateral to be posted and received for each date are based on the binomial tree in Exhibit VI-5 for the 3.80% receive-fixed swap in the inter-dealer market.

The upper table in Exhibit VI-6 shows the expected funding costs to be 0.0145 per 100 of notional principal; the lower table shows the expected funding benefit to be 0.0510. The FVA is -0.0365, indicating a net FVA gain to the commercial bank: $0.0145 - 0.0510 = -0.0365$. The key calculations are the expected cash collateral that is posted or received each year. Given that the Date-0 VND is $+3.7075$, the bank receives that amount in cash from the dealer and pays only the 1-year benchmark rate for use of those funds. The produces a Date-1 benefit at the end of the year in the lower table and no cost in the upper table. The amount of the benefit is the "haircut" that does not have to be paid to acquire the cash. In the money market, the bank pays the benchmark rate plus a credit spread that depends on the probability that the bank defaults and the loss severity. That benefit is 0.0165 per 100 of notional principal in present value terms: $3.7075 * 90\% * 0.50\% * 0.990099 = 0.0165$. Even though there are only two derivatives in the portfolio, it is assumed that the bank benefits when obtaining cash for use in other operations and having to pay only the benchmark rate to obtain that cash.

Exhibit VI-7 displays the projected postings and receipts of cash collateral on the receive-fixed hedge swap with dealer. The positive amounts are receipts of cash that generate funding benefits and the negative amounts are the postings of cash that lead to funding costs because of the "haircut" that needs to be paid to acquire funds in the money market. These are drawn from the swap values and net settlement payments in Exhibit VI-5. These are the calculations for Date 4:

At 8.8042% $-3.9638 - 2.7184 = -6.6822$

At 5.4190% $-1.5358 + (-2.7184 - 0.5694)/2 = -3.1797$

At 3.6324% $+0.1617 + (-0.5694 + 0.8711)/2 = 0.3126$

At 2.4349% $+1.3327 + (0.8711 + 1.8367)/2 = 2.6866$

At 1.6322% $+2.1330 + 1.8367 = 3.9697$

Exhibit VI-7: Projected Postings and Receipts of Cash Collateral

Date 0	Date 1	Date 2	Date 3	Date 4

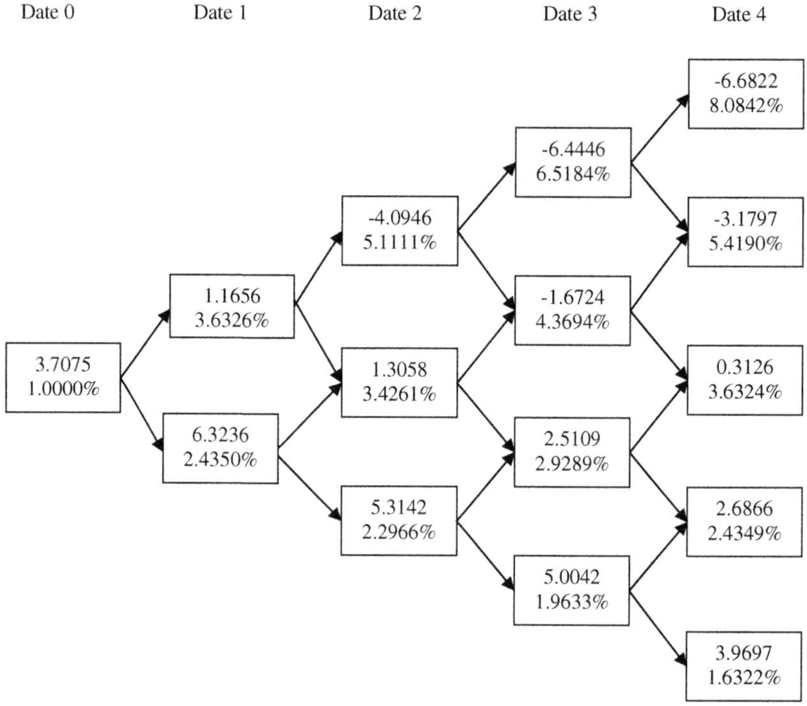

Note: Positive amounts are received cash collateral and negative amounts are posted cash collateral.

The expected postings and receipts of cash collateral in Exhibit VI-6 depend on the signs of the values in Exhibit VI-7. As with the calculation of CVA and DVA, the probabilities of attaining those nodes in the binomial tree are used to get the expected values. The expected amount of cash to be posted by the bank on Date 3 is 1.4327 per 100 of notional principal:

$$(0.125 * 6.4446) + (0.375 * 1.6724) + (0.375 * 0)$$
$$+(0.125 * 0) = 1.4327.$$

The first two terms are the negative values in Exhibit VI-7 for Date 3. The positive numbers revert to zero because those entail the receipt of cash collateral, resulting in a benefit rather than a cost. This leads to an expected funding cost on Date 4 of 0.0057 per 100 of notional principal as a present value: $1.4327*90\%*0.49254\%*0.894344 = 0.0057$. The cost is incurred because cash to meet the collateral requirement must be acquired by the bank in the money market at the market rate for its credit standing. The credit spread over the benchmark rate that the bank pays lenders is passed on to the swap trading desk in the form of the FVA. The reality that the bank does not issue debt at the benchmark rate is a cost to the business of derivatives market-making.

Similarly, the expected amount of cash to be received by the bank on Date 4 is 1.0370:

$$(0.0625 * 0) + (0.25 * 0) + (0.375 * 0.3126) * (0.25 * 2.6866)$$
$$+ (0.0625 * 3.9697) = 1.0370.$$

These are the positive values in Exhibit VI-7; the negative values revert to zero. This cash flow generates and expected benefit of 0.0039 on Date 5: $1.0370 * 90\% * 0.49007\% * 0.860968 = 0.0039$. The benefit arises from receiving cash and not having to pay the "haircut" — the bank is effectively borrowing funds at a below-market interest rate.

The FVA for the 5-year, collateralized, 3.80% received-fixed hedge swap is a present value of -0.0365, indicating a net FVA gain to the commercial bank because in this case the expected funding benefit exceeds the costs. Notice that formulated in this manner the FVA is a hybrid of the CVA and DVA. The pattern for expected collateral to be posted each date that is used to get the expected funding cost, that is, the upper table in Exhibit VI-6, is similar to the pattern for expected exposure to default by the corporate counterparty used to get the CVA in Exhibit VI-2. The pattern for the receipt of cash collateral (the lower table in Exhibit VI-6) is similar to the expected exposure to default by the bank used to get the DVA in Exhibit VI-2. The same credit risk parameters associated with the bank — the assumed probability of default and the recovery rate — are used to get both the FVA and the DVA.

In general, the value of a swap including the FVA is:

$$\text{Value}^{\text{SWAP}} = \text{VND} - \text{CVA} + \text{DVA} - \text{FVA} \qquad (1)$$

The 5-year, collateralized, 3.80% receive-fixed swap has a VND = +3.7075, CVA = 0, DVA = 0, and FVA = −0.0365. Overall, the value of the hedge swap is +3.7440.

$$\text{Value}^{\text{SWAP}} = +3.7075 - 0 + 0 - (-0.0365) = +3.7440$$

Recognizing the FVA gain on the hedge swap, the value of the derivatives portfolio is raised from 0.2253 per 100 of notional principal (= −3.4822+3.7075) to 0.2618(= −3.4822+3.7440). Notice that the value of the swap with the corporate counterparty is unchanged. In this example, the net funding cost or benefit applies to the hedge swap.

VI.4: Swap Portfolio Valuation Including FVA — Second Method

The second method to calculate FVA is to project the 1-year cost of funds in the money market using the benchmark rate for each node in the tree and the credit risk parameters. Given the assumptions about the bank's probability of default (POD) for each year and the recovery rate (RR), the market rate (MR) for the bank's 1-year money market debt relative to the benchmark rate (BR) can be estimated as follows:

$$(1 + \text{BR}) = [(1 - \text{POD}) * (1 + \text{MR})] + [\text{POD} * (1 + \text{MR}) * \text{RR}] \qquad (2)$$

The left-side of the equation is the return per dollar invested in the 1-year risk-free benchmark security. The right-side is the weighted average return on buying the bank's 1-year debt liability that pays the market rate, using the probability of default and no-default as the weights. Notice that as POD approaches zero and as RR approaches one, MR equals BR and the bank's credit spread becomes zero. Rearranging equation (2) gives an equation for the market rate given the other variables:

$$MR = \frac{BR + [POD * (1 - RR)]}{1 - [POD * (1 - RR)]} \tag{3}$$

This equation assumes risk-neutrality on the part of money market investors in that there is no term for risk aversion.

Exhibit VI-8 shows the binomial tree for the commercial bank's 1-year cost of funds based on its credit risk parameters: POD = 0.50% and RR = 10%. For instance, on Date 1 when the benchmark rate is 3.6326%, the bank's market rate is 4.1011% calculated using equation (3).

$$MR = \frac{0.036326 + [0.0050 * (1 - 0.10)]}{1 - [0.0050 * (1 - 0.10)]} = 0.041011$$

Exhibit VI-8: Binomial Forward Rate Tree for the Commercial Bank's 1-Year Money Market Rate

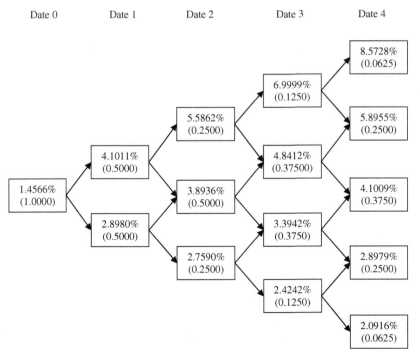

On Date 4 when the benchmark rate is 8.0842%, the bank's market for 1-year funds is 8.5728%.

$$MR = \frac{0.080842 + [0.0050 * (1 - 0.10)}{1 - [0.0050 * (1 - 0.10)]} = 0.085728$$

Notice that the credit spread increases with the level of the benchmark rate. It is 46.85 basis points in the first example (4.1011% − 3.6326% = 0.4685%) and 48.86 basis points in the second (8.5728% − 8.0842% = 0.4886%).

Exhibit VI-9 presents the tables used to calculate the FVA on the 3.80% hedge swap for the second method. The key calculations involve the expected cash collateral that is posted or received each year using the values in Exhibit VI-7. Given that the Date-0 VND is +3.7075, the bank receives that amount in cash from the dealer

Exhibit VI-9: Second Method to Calculate the Funding Costs and Benefits

Funding Costs

Date	Expected Funding Cost Per Year	Benchmark Discount Factor	PV of Funding Costs
1	0.0000	0.990099	0.0000
2	0.0000	0.960978	0.0000
3	0.0049	0.928023	0.0045
4	0.0068	0.894344	0.0061
5	0.0058	0.860968	0.0050
			0.0156

Funding Benefits

Date	Expected Funding Benefit Per Year	Benchmark Discount Factor	PV of Funding Benefit
1	0.0169	0.990099	0.0168
2	0.0174	0.960978	0.0167
3	0.0092	0.928023	0.0085
4	0.0073	0.894344	0.0065
5	0.0048	0.860968	0.0041
			0.0526

FVA = Funding Costs − Funding Benefits = 0.0156 − 0.0526 = −0.0370

and pays only the 1-year benchmark interest rate. That produces a Date-1 benefit in the lower table and no cost in the upper table. The amount of the benefit is the 0.0169 as of Date 1 at the end of the year: $3.7075 * (1.4566\% - 1.0000\%) = 0.0169$.

On Date 1 the bank expects to receive either 1.1656 or 6.3236 depending the 1-year benchmark rate going from 1.0000% up to 3.6326% or "down" to 2.4350%, with equal probabilities. The expected benefit as of Date 2 at the end of the year is 0.0174:

$$[0.5 * 1.1656 * (4.1011\% - 3.6326\%)]$$
$$+ [0.5 * 6.3236 * (2.8980\% - 2.4350\%)] = 0.0174$$

In each case, the benefit arises from the credit spread, that is, the difference between the market rate and the benchmark rate. For Date 3 the expected benefit is 0.0092:

$$[0.25 * 0 * (5.5862\% - 5.1111\%)]$$
$$+ [0.5 * 1.3058 * (3.8936\% - 3.4261\%)]$$
$$+ [0.25 * 5.3142 * (2.7590\% - 2.2966\%)] = 0.0092$$

Notice that 0 is entered in the first term because the value in Exhibit VI-7 is negative, indicating a cost.

The negative values in Exhibit VI-7 imply funding costs for the bank. The expected cost for Date 4 is 0.0068:

$$[0.125 * 6.4446 * (6.9999\% - 6.5184\%)]$$
$$+ [0.375 * 1.6724 * (4.4812\% - 4.3694\%)]$$
$$+ [0.375 * 0 * (3.3942\% - 2.9289\%)]$$
$$+ [0.125 * 0 * (2.4242\% - 1.9633\%)] = 0.0068.$$

The last two values are 0 because the positive amounts represent funding benefits. The expected funding cost for Date 5 is 0.0058:

$$[0.0625 * 6.6822 * (8.5728\% - 8.0842\%)]$$
$$+ [0.25 * 3.1797 * (5.8955\% - 5.4190\%)]$$

$$+ [0.375 * 0 * (4.1009\% - 3.6324\%)]$$
$$+ [0.25 * 0 * (2.8979\% - 2.4349\%)]$$
$$+ [0.0625 * 0 * (2.0916\% - 1.6322\%)] = 0.0058.$$

Using the second method, the overall expected funding cost is 0.0156 (per 100 of notional principal) and the funding benefit is 0.0526. Combined, the FVA is −0.0370, indicating a net funding benefit to the bank slightly higher than the result for the first method. The benefit arises because interest rates have decreased since the swap was initiated. The uncollateralized payer swap with the corporate counterparty is "out of the money" to the bank as it has negative fair value. However, the collateralized receiver swap with the dealer is "in the money". The receipt of cash collateral provides a benefit because the bank can use those funds in its operations and pay only the benchmark rate instead of its own market rate that reflects its credit risk parameters.

The small difference in the FVA results from the calculation methodology. In the first method, the "haircut" is based on the expected amount of cash collateral to be posted or received. That amount is the assumed principal on the 1-year security. In the second method, the market rate is projected, given the credit risk parameters, such that a money market investor's expected return matches that on the benchmark security, including both principal and interest. Including the interest explains why the second method is slightly higher. There are obviously many other assumptions that go into implementing FVA in practice. For instance, here it is assumed that the swap remains on the books of the bank for the remaining five years — and incurs five years' worth of funding benefits and costs. In reality, many swaps are terminated early. Therefore, the bank could assume some pattern of decline in the notional principal on the overall derivatives portfolio.

In the example, the FVA gain to the bank arises because the VND on the underlying pay-fixed swap with the corporate counterparty is negative. Market interest rates have come down since inception so the gain on received-fixed hedge swap offsets that negative value. This is all reversed if the legs to the underlying swap are opposite. If the commercial bank had entered a 3.75% receive-fixed swap with the corporation, the VND would be positive. Then the pay-fixed hedge swap would require posting cash collateral. The recognition of the net funding cost results in an FVA loss.

The key point is that the positions the bank has in collateralized swaps — and to funding costs and benefits — typically will be exogenously determined by demand for derivatives from its customers. Of course, the bank will have some influence on the types of derivatives that it emphasizes in its marketing programs but to a large extent the composition of its holdings is customer-driven.

VI.5: Study Questions

Assume that a commercial bank has only two interest rate swaps in its derivatives portfolio: (1) a 5-year, 4.40%, annual settlement, *uncollateralized*, receive-fixed swap with a corporate counterparty, and (2) a 5-year, 4.35%, annual settlement, *collateralized*, pay-fixed swap with a dealer. Both swaps were originated five years ago — the second swap as a hedge to the first. The notional principal on each swap is $25,000,000. The assumed credit risk parameters for the corporation and the commercial bank are conditional probabilities of default of 2.00% and 0.75%, respectively, and recovery rates of 40% and 20%.

(A) Calculate the fair value of the derivatives portfolio to the commercial bank including the CVA, DVA, and FVA using the first method for the FVA calculation.
(B) Calculate the fair value of the derivatives portfolio to the commercial bank including the CVA, DVA, and FVA using the second method for the FVA calculation.

VI.6: Answers to the Study Questions

(A) The first step is to calculate the fair value of the uncollateralized swap with the corporate counterparty. Exhibit VI-10 shows

Exhibit VI-10: Valuation of the 4.40%, 5-Year, Receive-Fixed Interest Rate Swap Assuming No Default

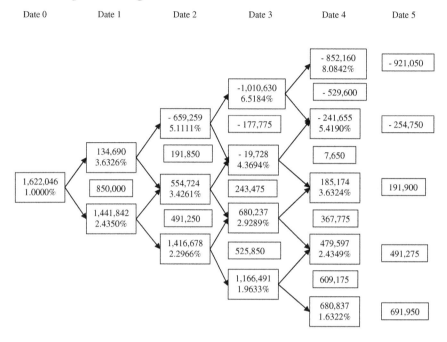

that the VND for the 4.40%, receive-fixed swap is $1,622,046 from the perspective of the commercial bank. Exhibit VI-11 displays the calculation of the CVA and DVA. Given that the swap has become an asset to the bank and the difference in the credit risk parameters, the CVA and DVA are quite imbalanced. The CVA (the risk of the corporation defaulting) is $43,445 and the DVA (the credit risk of the bank itself) is $3,204. Combined (and calculated on the spreadsheet), the net fair value of the swap is $1,581,804 (= $1,622,046 − $43,445 + $3,204).

The second step is the calculate the value of the 4.35%, pay-fixed collateralized swap with dealer. Exhibit VI-12 shows that the VND is −$1,564,115 from the perspective of the commercial bank. Because the swap is collateralized, we can assume that the CVA and DVA are zero. Therefore, the fair value of the swap is −$1,564,115.

Exhibit VI-11: CVA and DVA Calculations on the 4.40%, 5-Year, Interest Rate Swap

Credit Risk of the Fixed-Rate Payer, the Corporate Counterparty

Credit Risk Parameters: 2.00% Conditional Probability of Default, 40% Recovery Rate

Date	Expected Exposure	LGD	POD	Discount Factor	CVA
1	1,638,266	982,960	2.00000%	0.990099	19,465
2	925,119	555,071	1.96000%	0.960978	10,455
3	615,800	369,480	1.92080%	0.928023	6,586
4	462,476	277,486	1.88238%	0.894344	4,671
5	238,028	142,817	1.84474%	0.860968	2,268
			9.60792%		43,445

Credit Risk of the Fixed-Rate Receiver, the Commercial Bank

Credit Risk Parameters: 0.75% Conditional Probability of Default, 20% Recovery Rate

Date	Expected Exposure	LGD	POD	Discount Factor	DVA
1	0	0	0.75000%	0.990099	0
2	116,852	93,482	0.74438%	0.960978	669
3	148,551	118,841	0.73879%	0.928023	815
4	212,017	169,614	0.73325%	0.894344	1,112
5	121,253	97,003	0.72775%	0.860968	608
			3.69417%		3,204

Exhibit VI-12: Valuation of the 4.35%, 5-Year, Pay-Fixed Interest Rate Swap Assuming No Default

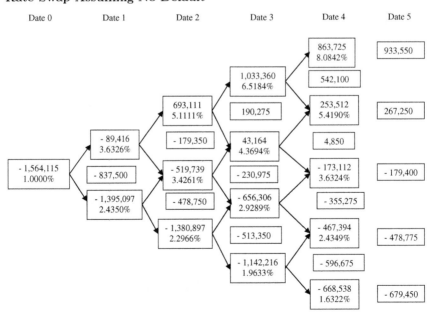

Exhibit VI-13: Projected Postings and Receipts of Cash Collateral

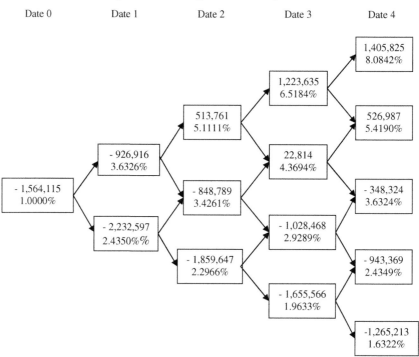

Note: Positive amounts are received cash collateral and negative amounts are posted collateral.

The value of the swaps portfolio includes the FVA that arises from the collateralized hedge swap. Exhibit VI-13 shows the expected receipts and postings of cash collateral. These are mostly postings of collateral (the negative amounts) because the payer swap is a liability to the bank and an asset to the dealer. Exhibit VI-14 shows the FVA calculations. The present values of expected funding costs and benefits are $28,552 and $2,653, respectively. When calculated on a spreadsheet, the net FVA is $25,900 using the first method.

Exhibit VI-14: First Method to Calculate the Funding Costs and Benefits

Expected Funding Costs

Date	Expected Posting of Cash Collateral	Loss Severity	POD	Discount Factor	Expected Funding Costs
1	1,564,115	80%	0.75000%	0.990099	9,292
2	1,579,757	80%	0.74438%	0.960978	9,040
3	889,306	80%	0.73879%	0.928023	4,878
4	592,621	80%	0.73325%	0.894344	3,109
5	445,540	80%	0.72775%	0.860968	2,233
					28,552

Expected Funding Benefits

Date	Expected Receipt of Cash Collateral	Loss Severity	POD	Discount Factor	Expected Funding Benefit
1	0	80%	0.75000%	0.990099	0
2	0	80%	0.74438%	0.960978	0
3	128,440	80%	0.73879%	0.928023	704
4	161,510	80%	0.73325%	0.894344	847
5	219,611	80%	0.72775%	0.860968	1,101
					2,653

FVA = Funding Costs – Funding Benefits = 28,552 – 2,653 = 25,900

Note: The columns for the expected posting and receipt of cash collateral refer to the previous date. For example, the bank posts $1,564,115 in cash collateral on Date 0. That generates an expected funding cost on Date 1. In present value terms, that benefit is $9,292.

The value of the derivatives portfolio composed of the two swaps is −$8,211.

$$\$1,581,804 - \$1,564,115 - \$25,900 = -\$8,211$$

The most likely reason for the negative value for the portfolio is that the credit quality of the corporate countparty has deteriorated since the swap was entered five years ago. That increases the CVA as its probability of default has gone up or the assumed recovery rate has gone down. Another possibility is that the FVA was not factored into the original pricing of the swap that set the fixed rate to be 4.40%. Now that the FVA is recognized, the portfolio has less value due to the net funding costs.

(B) The second method to calculate FVA entails projecting 1-year money market interest rates for the commercial bank using its credit risk parameters and equation (3). This tree is presented in Exhibit VI-15. The differences between these money market rates and the benchmark rates then drive the funding costs and benefits given the expected receipts and postings of cash collateral in Exhibit VI-13. The tables in Exhibit V-16 indicate expected funding costs of $29,642 and benefit of $2,899. The net FVA is $26,743 using the second method. The value for the derivatives portfolio is −$9,054(= $1,581,804 − $1,564,115 − $26,743).

Exhibit VI-15: Binomial Forward Rate Tree for the Commercial Bank's 1-Year Money Market Rate

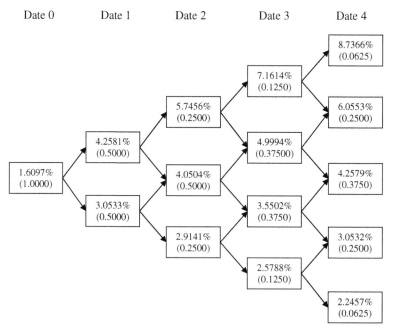

Exhibit VI-16: Second Method to Calculate the Funding Costs and Benefits

Funding Costs

Date	Expected Funding Cost Per Year	Benchmark Discount Factor	PV of Funding Costs
1	9,536	0.990099	9,441
2	9,801	0.960978	9,419
3	5,520	0.928023	5,123
4	3,670	0.894344	3,282
5	2,760	0.860968	2,377
			29,642

Funding Benefits

Date	Expected Funding Benefit Per Year	Benchmark Discount Factor	PV of Funding Benefit
1	0	0.990099	0
2	0	0.960978	0
3	815	0.928023	756
4	1,037	0.894344	928
5	1,412	0.860968	1,215
			2,899

FVA = Funding Costs – Funding Benefits = \$29,642 – 2,899 = \$26,743

Endnotes

1. This example is based on the discussion of FVA in a publication by KPMG (2013). An earlier version of this chapter is "Understanding CVA, DVA, and FVA: Examples of Interest Rate Swap Valuation"; see Smith (2015).
2. See Adams and Smith (2013) for further motivations for this type of asset-driven liability structure.

Chapter VII

Structured Notes

The binomial forward rate tree model is quite general and can be used to value a wide range of debt securities and interest rate derivatives. This chapter extends the analysis to structured notes, in particular, to an inverse floating-rate note and a bear floater.[1] These securities were introduced in the 1980s during a wave of financial market innovation, motivated in part by the extreme interest rate volatility experienced in the U.S. in those years and the diversity of opinion about future rate movements. Inverse floaters, also known as bull floaters, are attractive to investors who expect interest rates to be low, hence a bull market for bond prices. Bear floaters are attractive to investors who expect rates to be going up, a bear market for bond prices.

VII.1: An Inverse (Bull) Floater

Suppose that a 5-year, inverse floating-rate note pays an interest rate of 6.50% *minus* the 1-year benchmark bond rate, subject to a minimum of 0%. The annual interest payments are deemed to be "inverse" because they go up then the reference rate goes down, and vice versa. The issuer is assumed to have a conditional default probability of 0.75% and a recovery rate of 40% per year. In the past, some structured notes such as these were issued by federal agencies having AAA credit ratings. Investors were interested in an aggressive "interest rate play" and not a bet on credit risk, which would have drawn them instead to the high-yield corporate bond market. The Orange County Investment Pool, and its bankruptcy in 1994, became infamous because of its strategy of using leverage via the repo markets to build a large bond portfolio composed in part of inverse floaters.

Exhibit VII-1 presents the binomial tree used to calculate the VND for the inverse floater and the table to get the CVA given the credit risk parameters. Typical of floating-rate notes, the interest payments are in arrears. The Date-1 payment is 5.50 per 100 in par value because the Date-0 rate is 1.0000%: $(6.5000\% - 1.0000\%) * 100 = 5.50$. If the 1-year benchmark bond rate is at the 2.2966% node on

Exhibit VII-1: Valuation of a 5-Year, Inverse Floating-Rate Note Paying 6.50% Minus the 1-Year Rate, Subject to a 0% Minimum

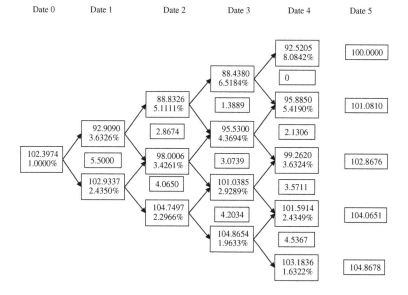

Credit Risk Parameters: 0.75% Conditional Probability of Default, 40% Recovery Rate

Date	Expected Exposure	LGD	POD	Discount Factor	CVA
1	103.4213	62.0528	0.75000%	0.990099	0.4608
2	100.8620	60.5172	0.74438%	0.960978	0.4329
3	100.8111	60.4867	0.73879%	0.928023	0.4147
4	101.5291	60.9175	0.73325%	0.894344	0.3995
5	102.6661	61.5997	0.72775%	0.860968	0.3860
			3.69417%		2.0938

Fair Value = 102.3974 − 2.0938 = 100.3035   (100.30351025)

Date 2, the Date-3 payment is 4.2034 [= (6.5000% − 2.2966%) ∗ 100]. However, if the 1-year rate rises to 6.5184% on Date 3, the *non-negativity* constraint is binding. A negative interest rate would imply that the investor owes an interest payment to the issuer. Therefore, the payment on Date 4 is zero. The constraint also is binding at the top of the tree on Date 4 when the 1-year rate is 8.0842%. Then the investor receives only the redemption of par value at maturity on Date 5.

The VND for the inverse floater is 102.3974, the CVA is 2.0938, and the fair value is 100.3035 per 100 of par value. Clearly, the buyer of the inverse floater is hoping that 1-year rates remain in the lower half of the tree. Suppose that rates track the lowest path, so that the sequence of interest payments is 5.5000, 4.0650, 4.2034, 4.5367, and 4.8678. The realized internal rate of return would be 4.5731%, calculated as the solution for "i" and assuming no default:

$$100.3035 = \frac{5.5000}{(1+i)^1} + \frac{4.0650}{(1+i)^2} + \frac{4.2034}{(1+i)^3} + \frac{4.5367}{(1+i)^4} + \frac{104.8678}{(1+i)^5},$$
$$i = 0.045731$$

That would be an impressive outcome–the interest income and overall rate of return are high relative to prevailing relatively low benchmark money market rates.

Exhibit VII-2 repeats the valuation exercise for 10% volatility. This is the same tree that is first used in Chapter II to assess the impact of volatility on bond valuation. The values for the inverse floater for 20% and 10% volatility are summarized in the following table:

Volatility Assumption	VND	CVA	Fair Value
20%, Exhibit VII-1	102.3974	2.0938	100.3035
10%, Exhibit VII-2	102.3172	2.0927	100.2244
Difference	0.0802	0.0011	0.0791

Notice that the VND is changed, going down from 102.3974 to 102.3172 for the lower volatility. The fair value is also lower, going

Exhibit VII-2: Valuation of the Inverse Floating-Rate Note for 10% Volatility

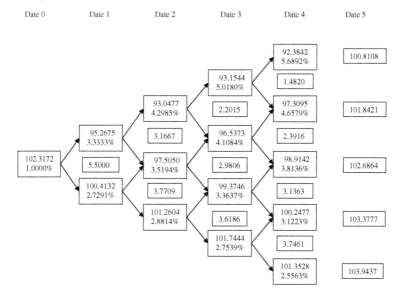

Credit Risk Parameters: 0.75% Conditional Probability of Default, 40% Recovery Rate

Date	Expected Exposure	LGD	POD	Discount Factor	CVA
1	103.3403	62.0042	0.75000%	0.990099	0.4604
2	100.7983	60.4790	0.74438%	0.960978	0.4326
3	100.7746	60.4648	0.73879%	0.928023	0.4146
4	101.5047	60.9028	0.73325%	0.894344	0.3994
5	102.6095	61.5657	0.72775%	0.860968	0.3858
			3.69417%		2.0927

Fair Value = 102.3172 − 2.0927 = 100.2244

from 100.3035 to 100.2244 and including the small, offsetting change in the CVA. Clearly, the impact on the fair value comes mostly from the change in the VND.

The volatility effect on the VND of the inverse floater can be explained by *reverse engineering* its cash flows to identify the presence of an embedded option. Suppose that a 5-year, 3.25% fixed-rate bond issued by the same entity exists. Also, assume that the investor can enter a 5-year, 3.25% receiver swap, paying the 1-year rate. In addition, assume that a 5-year interest rate cap at a strike rate of 6.50% is available.

Using the arithmetic of financial engineering, a long position in the inverse floater (indicated by the "+" sign) can be interpreted as owning the fixed-rate bond, selling the interest rate swap as the fixed-rate receiver, and buying the cap:

$$+ \text{Inverse Floater} = + \text{Fixed-Rate Bond} - \text{Receiver Swap}$$
$$+ \text{Interest Rate Cap} \tag{1}$$

The interest payments on the 3.25% bond and 3.25% fixed-rate leg of the swap provide the 6.50% cash inflows and the floating-rate leg of the swap represents the 1-year rate outflow. The role of the 6.50% cap to protect against the 1-year rate rising above 6.50% — it effectively is the equivalent of the non-negativity constraint in the inverse floater. The notional principals on the swap and the floor match the par values for the floater and the fixed-rate bond.

To illustrate the financial engineering, Exhibits VII-3, VII-4, and VII-5 show the VND calculations for the 3.25% fixed-rate bond, the

Exhibit VII-3: VND Calculation of the 3.25% Fixed-Rate Bonds

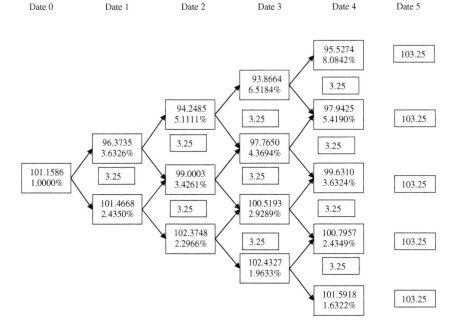

| Date 0 | Date 1 | Date 2 | Date 3 | Date 4 | Date 5 |

Exhibit VII-4: VND Calculation of the 3.25% Receive-Fixed Interest Rate Swap

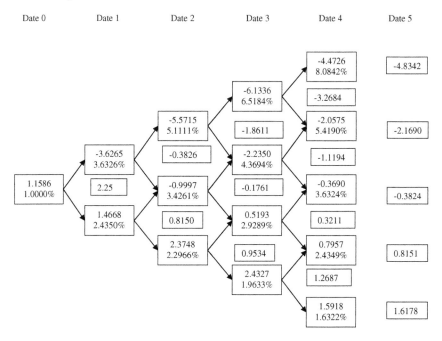

| Date 0 | Date 1 | Date 2 | Date 3 | Date 4 | Date 5 |

3.25% receive-fixed interest rate swap, and the 6.50% interest rate cap. The VNDs for the 3.25% bond and 3.25% receiver swap are 101.1586 and 1.1586, respectively. Their binomial trees demonstrate once again that, barring counterparty credit risk, a receive-fixed swap can be interpreted as a long position in a fixed-rate bond and a short position in a floating-rate note paying the 1-year benchmark rate. The swap value at each node in Exhibit VII-4 is the value in Exhibit VII-3 minus 100; see Exhibit V-12 in Chapter V for the demonstration that the floater has a value of 100 at each node in the binomial tree. The VND for the 6.50% cap is 0.0801. The sum of the VNDs for these components is 102.3973 (= 101.1586 + 1.1586 + 0.0801), which matches the VND for the inverse floater. [The match is exact when the values obtained on the spreadsheets are linked and not rounded to four digits.]

The VNDs for both the fixed-rate bond and the interest rate swap are independent of the volatility assumption because the value given

Exhibit VII-5: VND Calculation of the 6.50% Interest Rate Cap

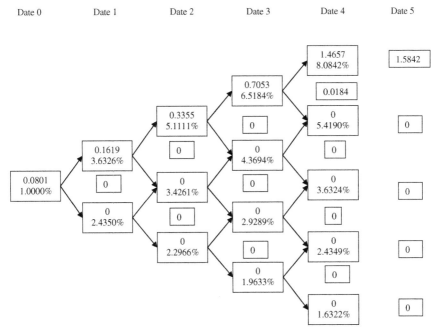

no default can be obtained directly from the benchmark discount factors. However, the VND for the implicit interest rate cap clearly depends on the assumed volatility. As volatility goes down from 20% to 10%, the value of the 6.50% cap on the 1-year rate goes down from 0.0801 to zero. That is because in highest rate achieved in the tree for 10% volatility is 5.6892%. Given a strike rate of 6.50%, there is no node that leads to a payoff to the cap owner.

Equation (1) suggests that an investor might choose between buying the inverse floater outright or building a derivatives-based portfolio to create the same cash flows, assuming no default. One advantage of the structured note is simpler credit risk analysis (other advantages might be in pricing relative to the portfolio, as well as in financial reporting requirements and tax treatment). The fair value of the inverse floater reflects only the CVA of the issuer. If the portfolio is purchased, the fair value includes the credit risk on the bond plus the fair value of the swap, which includes both the CVA of the counterparty and the DVA of the investor. The fair value of the cap depends on the writer of the derivative, perhaps the same or some other commercial bank. Complicating the analysis further is the *correlation* of the default probabilities across the various entities — a topic well beyond the scope of this introduction to valuation.

The effective duration and convexity of the inverse floater are calculated from the valuations using the bumped binomial trees first shown in Exhibits II-9 and II-11 in Chapter II and maintaining the same credit risk parameters. The following table summarizes these results for 20% volatility.

	Fair Value
MV_0	100.30351025
MV_+	99.85668556
MV_-	100.75896927

The MV_0 is from Exhibit VII-1, extended to eight digits for needed precision in the calculations. The MV_+ and MV_- binomial trees and tables are shown in Exhibits VII-6 and VII-7. As this is an inverse floater, all the values and payments are lower when the benchmark par curve is bumped up and higher when it is bumped down.

The effective duration for this 5-year debt security is 8.9955 and its BPV is 0.0902284 per 100 in par value.

$$\text{Effective Duration} = \frac{100.75896927 - 99.85668556}{2 * 0.0005 * 100.30351025} = 8.9955$$
$$\text{BPV} = 8.9955 * 100.30351025 * 0.0001 = 0.0902284$$

These risk statistics explain the potential attraction to the inverse floater from bullish investors anticipating lower future benchmark bond interest rates. The price sensitivity is almost double that of a fixed-rate bond having the same time to maturity. The 5-year, 4.25% fixed-rate bond in Exhibit V-15 has an effective duration of 4.5245 and a BPV of 0.0450104.

Exhibit VII-6: Valuation of the Inverse Floating-Rate Note After a 5-Basis-Point Upward Shift in the Benchmark Par Curve

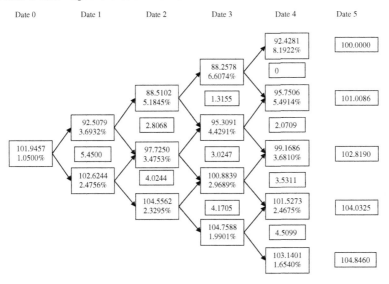

Credit Risk Parameters: 0.75% Conditional Probability of Default, 40% Recovery Rate

Date	Expected Exposure	LGD	POD	Discount Factor	CVA
1	103.0162	61.8097	0.75000%	0.990099	0.4590
2	100.5447	60.3268	0.74438%	0.960978	0.4315
3	100.5833	60.3500	0.73879%	0.928023	0.4138
4	101.3952	60.8371	0.73325%	0.894344	0.3990
5	102.6203	61.5722	0.72775%	0.860968	0.3858
			3.69417%		2.0890

Fair Value = 101.9457 – 2.0890 = 99.8567   (99.85668556)

An impressive risk statistic for the inverse floater is its effective convexity of 344.3280.

Effective Convexity

$$= \frac{(100.75896927) + (99.85668556) - (2 * 100.30351025)}{(0.0005)^2 * (100.30351025)}$$

$$= 344.3280$$

In contrast, 4.25% fixed-rate bond has an effective convexity of only 25.4198. The owner of this inverse floater is "buying almost twice as much duration and over 13 times as much convexity"!

Exhibit VII-7: Valuation of the Inverse Floating-Rate Note After a 5-Basis-Point Downwardward Shift in the Benchmark Par Curve

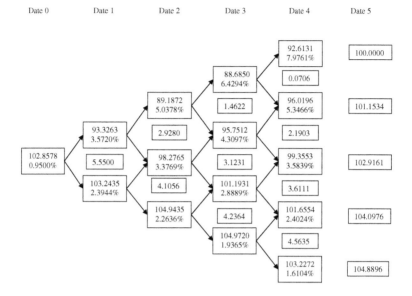

Credit Risk Parameters: 0.75% Conditional Probability of Default, 40% Recovery Rate

Date	Expected Exposure	LGD	POD	Discount Factor	CVA
1	103.8349	62.3009	0.75000%	0.990099	0.4626
2	101.1877	60.7126	0.74438%	0.960978	0.4343
3	101.0474	60.6285	0.73879%	0.928023	0.4157
4	101.6718	61.0031	0.73325%	0.894344	0.4000
5	102.7119	61.6271	0.72775%	0.860968	0.3861
			3.69417%		2.0988

Fair Value = 102.8578 − 2.0988 = 100.7590   (100.75896927)

VII.2: A Bear Floater

A bear floater can be analyzed in the same manner. Consider a floating-rate note that pays annually in arrears *two times* the 1-year benchmark bond yield *minus* 2.50%, subject to a minimum of 0%. The issuer is the same entity as for the inverse floater — the assumed conditional default probability is 0.75% and the recovery rate is 40% for each year. This security clearly appeals to an investor expecting higher money market rates because interest income will rise at twice the pace as an otherwise comparable traditional floating-rate note.

Exhibit VII-8: Valuation of a 5-Year, Bear Floating-Rate Note Paying Two Times the 1-Year Rate Minus 2.50%, Subject to a 0% Minimum

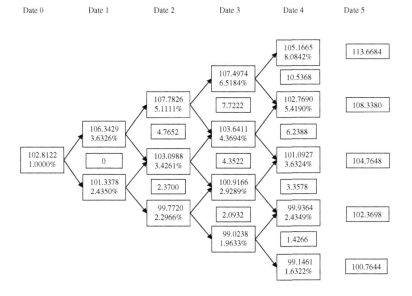

Credit Risk Parameters: 0.75% Conditional Probability of Default, 40% Recovery Rate

Date	Expected Exposure	LGD	POD	Discount Factor	CVA
1	103.8404	62.3042	0.75000%	0.990099	0.4627
2	107.0057	64.2034	0.74438%	0.960978	0.4593
3	107.1543	64.2926	0.73879%	0.928023	0.4408
4	106.4498	63.8699	0.73325%	0.894344	0.4188
5	105.3658	63.2195	0.72775%	0.860968	0.3961
			3.69417%		2.1777

Fair Value = 102.8122 – 2.1777 = 100.6346   (100.63456866)

Exhibit VII-8 displays the valuation of the bear floater. The non-negativity constraint is binding at issuance because the Date-0 rate is 1.00% [and $(2*1.00\% - 2.50\%)*100 = -0.50$]. Therefore, the Date-1 interest payment is zero. If on Date 1 the rate goes up to 3.6326%, the Date-2 payment is 4.7652 [$= (2 * 3.6326\% - 2.50\%) * 100$]. The VND for the security is 102.8122, the CVA is 2.1777, and the fair value is 100.6346. [Recall that all calculations are carried out on a spreadsheet and the rounded results are reported.] The potential benefit from owning the bear floater is apparent if rates track a path in the upper half of the tree. For instance, if rates track the topmost path, the realized annual internal rate of return would be 6.7515%, even with the first payment of zero.

$$100.6346 = \frac{0}{(1+i)^1} + \frac{4.7652}{(1+i)^2} + \frac{7.7222}{(1+i)^3} + \frac{10.5368}{(1+i)^4} + \frac{113.6684}{(1+i)^5},$$

$$i = 0.067515$$

Of course, given the assumptions about rate movements in the model, the probability of achieving that rate of return is only 0.0625.

The bear floater can be reverse engineered to be the combination of a straight FRN paying the 1-year rate flat and a pay-fixed interest rate swap, plus two interest rate floor contracts.

$$+ \text{Bear Floater} = +\text{Straight FRN} + \text{Payer Swap}$$

$$+ 2 \text{ Interest Rate Floors} \qquad (2)$$

The straight FRN provides one interest payment based on the 1-year benchmark bond rate, the receive-floating leg of the pay-fixed swap provides the other. The fixed-rate leg that is paid on the swap needs to be 2.50% to complete the $(2 * 1\text{-year Rate} -2.50\%)$ payment formula for the bear floater. The two interest rate floors each have a strike rate of 1.25% to maintain non-negativity. Note that each floor has a notional principal equal to the swap and the par values for the floater and the FRN. Instead, there could be just one floor having twice the notional principal.

Exhibits VII-9 and VII-10 display the binomial trees to the VNDs for the 2.50% payer swap and the 1.25% floor. These are 2.3172 and 0.2475. The swap has positive value to the fixed-rate payer because 2.50% is below the going market rate of 3.00%. The floor has such a low value because it is "in the money" only once, when the initial benchmark 1-year rate is 1.0000%. The combined value for the portfolio that duplicates the cash flows on the bear floater is 102.8122 $(= 100 + 2.3172 + 2 * 0.2475)$, matching the result for VND shown in Exhibit VII-8. Of course, the fair values of the explicit bear floater and the replicating portfolio likely will differ depending on the credit risk parameters of the counterparties.

The effective duration and convexity statistics for the bear floater are interesting. Exhibits VII-11 and VII-12 show the calculations for

Exhibit VII-9: VND Calculation of the 2.50% Pay-Fixed Interest Rate Swap

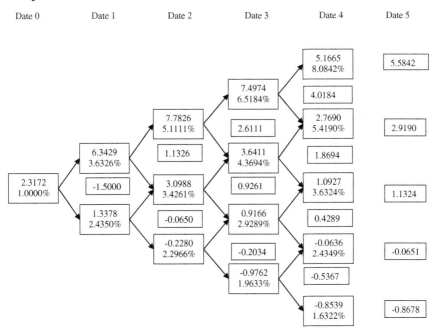

the 5-basis-point bumps in the benchmark par curve. The following table summarizes the results the for 8-digit fair values:

	Fair Value
MV_0	100.63456866
MV_+	100.75976624
MV_-	100.50882458

The effective duration for bear floater is -2.4936 and its BPV is -0.025094 per 100 in par value.

$$\text{Effective Duration} = \frac{100.50882458 - 100.75976624}{2 * 0.0005 * 100.63456866} = -2.4936$$

$$\text{BPV} = -2.4936 * 100.63456866 * 0.0001 = -0.025094$$

Exhibit VII-10: VND Calculation of the 1.25% Interest Rate Floor

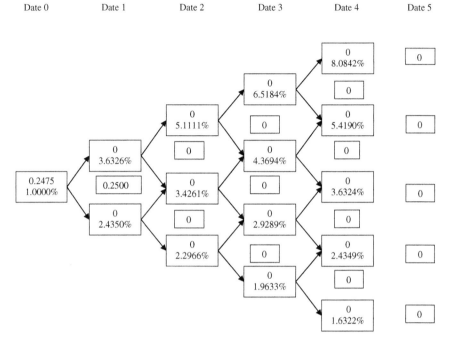

Negative duration is expected for a bear floater because, as seen in Exhibit VII-8, its interest payments increase by more than the increase in the 1-year benchmark rates. Notice that in equation (2) the implicit payer swap has negative duration — that is large enough to offset the positive duration of the two interest rate floors and the duration of the straight floater, which is close to zero. The effective convexity for the bear floater is -21.7221.

Effective Convexity

$$= \frac{(100.50882458) + (100.75976624) - (2 * 100.63456866)}{(0.0005)^2 * (100.63456866)}$$

$$= -21.7221$$

Structured notes have the potential to change the overall interest rate risk profile of a bond portfolio in significant ways. Adding inverse floaters increases duration and convexity; buying bear floaters

Exhibit VII-11: Valuation of the Bear Floater After a 5-Basis-Point Upward Shift in the Benchmark Par Curve

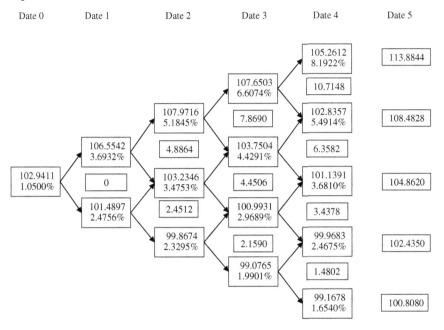

Credit Risk Parameters: 0.75% Conditional Probability of Default, 40% Recovery Rate

Date	Expected Exposure	LGD	POD	Discount Factor	CVA
1	104.0220	62.4132	0.75000%	0.990099	0.4635
2	107.2458	64.3475	0.74438%	0.960978	0.4603
3	107.3520	64.4112	0.73879%	0.928023	0.4416
4	106.6028	63.9617	0.73325%	0.894344	0.4194
5	105.4710	63.2826	0.72775%	0.860968	0.3965
			3.69417%		2.1813

Fair Value = 102.9411 − 2.1813 = 100.7598   (100.75976624)

decreases them. That is because an inverse floater contains an embedded receiver swap that has positive duration and convexity and a bear floater contains an embedded payer swap that has negative risk statistics. Moreover, the impact can be multiplied by adding to the coefficients in the payment formulas. For instance, a "leveraged" inverse floater could pay 12% minus *two times* the 1-year rate (the Orange County Investment Pool owned some of these too); a "big bear" floater could pay *three times* the 1-year rate minus 6%. The possibilities are endless.

Exhibit VII-12: Valuation of the Bear Floater After a 5-Basis-Point Downwardward Shift in the Benchmark Par Curve

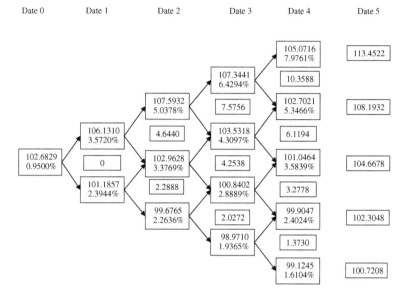

Credit Risk Parameters: 0.75% Conditional Probability of Default, 40% Recovery Rate

Date	Expected Exposure	LGD	POD	Discount Factor	CVA
1	103.6583	62.1950	0.75000%	0.990099	0.4618
2	106.7652	64.0591	0.74438%	0.960978	0.4582
3	106.9565	64.1739	0.73879%	0.928023	0.4400
4	106.2968	63.7781	0.73325%	0.894344	0.4182
5	105.2607	63.1564	0.72775%	0.860968	0.3957
			3.69417%		2.1740

Fair Value = 102.6829 − 2.1740 = 100.5088   (100.50882458)

VII.3: Study Questions

(A) Suppose that an aggressive institutional investor has a strongly held view on the prospective path for future 1-year benchmark interest rates. In particular, the view is that rates will be rising by more than is generally expected for the next two years (on Dates 1 and 2) and that rates will be lower than generally expected in the subsequent two years (on Dates 3 and 4). This investor is required to hold high-credit quality securities and is not allowed to directly enter derivative contracts like interest rate swaps, caps, and floors.

An investment banker working with the institutional investor has arranged for a federal agency to issue a novel structured note nicknamed a "bear to bull transformer". This 5-year note makes annual interest payments according to this schedule: (1) on Dates 1, 2, and 3 the payment is based on a formula of $(3 * 1\text{-year Benchmark Rate} - 6\%)$, and (3) on Dates 4 and 5 the payment is based on $(12\% - 2 * 1\text{-year Benchmark Rate})$. A non-negativity constraint assures a minimum rate of 0%. The federal agency can be assumed to have a conditional default probability of 0.10% and a recovery rate of 40% for each year.

Calculate the fair value for the "bear to bull transformer" per 100 of par value assuming constant 20% volatility for the 1-year benchmark rate.

(B) The investment bank and the federal agency enter a package of interest rate derivatives to transform the "bear to bull transformer" to a synthetic 3% fixed-rate debt liability. Identify the package of interest rate swaps, caps, and floor that accomplish this feat.

VII.4: Answers to the Study Questions

(A) Exhibit VII-13 shows the binomial tree and the credit risk table for the "bear to bull transformer." The interest payment is zero on Date 1 because the non-negativity contraint is binding: $(3 * 1.000\% - 6\%) * 100 = -3.0000$. If the 1-year benchmark rate is 5.1111% on Date 2, the interest payment due on Date 3 is 9.3333 per 100 of par value: $(3 * 5.1111\% - 6\%) * 100 = 9.3333$. If the rate is 2.9289% on Date 3, the payment at the end of the year is 6.1422: $(12\% - 2 * 2.9289\%) * 100 = 6.1422$. The non-negativity contraint is once again binding on Date 4 if the rate is 6.5184% on Date 3: $(12\% - 2 * 6.5184\%) * 100 = -1.0368$. It also is binding on Date 5 at the top node in the tree as the note essentially becomes a zero-coupon bond.

Exhibit VII-13: Valuation of a 5-Year, Bear to Bull Transformer Structured Note, Subject to a 0% Minimum

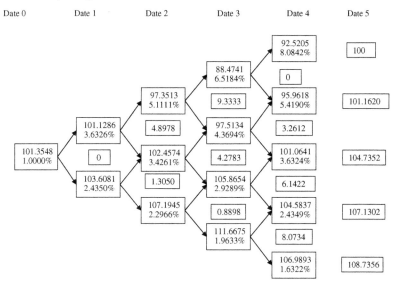

Credit Risk Parameters: 0.10% Conditional Probability of Default, 40% Recovery Rate

Date	Expected Exposure	LGD	POD	Discount Factor	CVA
1	102.3683	61.4210	0.10000%	0.990099	0.0608
2	105.4666	63.2799	0.09990%	0.960978	0.0607
3	105.9797	63.5878	0.09980%	0.928023	0.0589
4	105.0402	63.0241	0.09970%	0.894344	0.0562
5	104.3947	62.6368	0.09960%	0.860968	0.0537
			0.49900%		0.2904

Fair Value = 101.3548 – 0.2904 = 101.0644

The VND for the structured note is 101.3548 on Date 0. Given the assumption about the credit risk of the federal agency, the probability of default over the five years to maturity is only 0.49900%. The CVA is 0.2904 and fair value is 101.0644(= 101.3548 − 0.2904) per 100 of par value.

(B) The federal agency needs to enter a 3-year payer swap with the investment bank and buy 3-year interest rate floors to transform the "bear to bull transformer" into a synthetic 3% fixed-rate debt liability for the first three years. To be specific, the federal agency enters three swaps to pay 3% fixed and to receive the 1-year benchmark rate. Each swap has a notional principal equal to the par value of the structured note (or one swap having a notional principal three times the par value of the note). The three interest rate floors have a strike rate of 2% and, like the swaps, a notional principal equal to the note's par value.

To convert the final two years to a fixed rate, the federal agency enters two *forward-starting* receiver swaps with the investment bank and buys two caps. On a forward-starting derivative, the terms are set in advance at Date 0 but the contracts and the settlement payments are deferred until a future date. These could be named a "3 × 5" (or "3y2y") forward contracts because they are 2-year contracts deferred for three years. The 1-year benchmark rate observed on Date 3 determines the Date-4 payment; the rate on Date 4 determines the Date-5 payment. The federal agency needs to receive a fixed rate of 4.50% on two swaps and to buy two interest rate caps at a strike rate of 6.00%. The notional principals match the par value of the note.

Exhibit VII-14 shows the cash flows on the "bear to bull transformer" and the derivatives for a range of levels for the 1-year benchmark rate. Whatever rate is revealed, the *all-in* (meaning inclusive of the derivatives) interest payment sums to 3 per 100 of par value and notional principal.

While not asked in the question, the binomial tree model could be used to calculate the VND for the swaps, caps, and floors. Then given assumptions about the credit risk parameters of the federal agency and the investment bank, the fair values for the derivatives are obtained. Adding those to the fair value of the structured note gives the total present value for the portfolio. The 5-year cost of funds to the federal agency is the internal rate of return on the present value and the synthetically constructed 3% fixed coupon payments plus the redemption of principal at maturity. This all-in cost of funds should be lower than the yield to maturity on the agency's traditional 5-year fixed-rate bond offerings. If not, don't do it!

Exhibit VII-14: Converting the "Bear to Bull Transformer" Into a Synthetic Fixed-Rate Debt Liability

Dates 1, 2, and 3

1-Year Rate	Structured Note $3 * \text{Rate} - 6\%$	3 Pay-Fixed Swaps at 3%	3 Floors at 2%	All-In Cost per 100 of Par Value
0%	0	9	−6	3
3%	3	0	0	3
6%	12	−9	0	3
9%	21	−18	0	3
12%	30	−27	0	3

Dates 4 and 5

1-Year Rate	Structured Note $12\% - 2 * \text{Rate}$	2 Receive-Fixed Swaps at 4.50%	2 Caps at 6%	All-In Cost per 100 of Par Value
0%	12	−9	0	3
3%	6	−3	0	3
6%	0	3	0	3
9%	0	9	−6	3
12%	0	15	−12	3

Endnote

1. For an early and more theoretical examination of these securities, see Smith (1988).

Chapter VIII

Summary

This introduction to the valuation of debt securities and interest rate derivatives is an attempt to characterize the workings of the complex models used in practice by means of a simple, "artisanal" model of interest rate dynamics to obtain a value assuming no default and a separate, tabular calculation for the adjustments due to credit risk and funding costs. A novel aspect to the presentation is a link between the values in the binomial forward rate tree and the expected exposure to credit risk. While it is a caricature of its real-world counterparts, the binomial model of benchmark rates and CVA/DVA/FVA tables reveal some of the key assumptions that need to be made in the valuation process — for instance, the underlying stochastic process for the level and volatility of interest rates, collateralization, the probability of default, and the recovery rate if default occurs.

The key observations are:

- The XVA (including CVA, DVA, FVA, KVA, LVA, TVA, and MVA) are a series of valuation adjustments introduced since the financial crisis to identify the various factors that go into valuing debt securities and interest rate derivatives. The models used in practice to calculate the XVA are mathematically complex.

- The value of a default-risk-free (benchmark) bond is independent of the volatility assumption and can be calculated using (1) the series of discount factors, spot rates, or forward rates, or (2) via the binomial tree for forward short-term (here 1-year) benchmark rates. Both the discount factors and the binomial tree are derived from the coupon rates and prices on the benchmark bonds under the assumption of no arbitrage.
- The same value for a benchmark bond is obtained via the binomial tree using backward induction and using pathwise valuation.
- Credit risk is summarized by: (1) the spread over the yield to maturity on a risk-free benchmark bond, or (2) a credit valuation adjustment (the CVA/DVA) to the value of the bond if it were risk-free (the VND). The spread captures the credit risk as an annual rate over the lifetime of the bond; the CVA/DVA captures the credit risk in terms of present value. The fair value of the risky debt security is the VND minus the CVA/DVA.
- The fair value of a corporate bond to the investor is VND minus CVA; the value to the issuer is VND minus DVA. In principle, CVA equals DVA because the credit risk is unilateral. However, accounting rules might allow for different treatment of CVA and DVA in financial reports.
- The primary credit risk parameters are the conditional probability of default, recovery rate, and expected exposure to loss. The default probability and recovery rate are treated as exogenously determined in this book; the expected exposure is based on the binomial tree model and depends on the assumed interest rate volatility.
- When benchmark bond yields rise or fall, the change in the fair value of a corporate bond is less than the change in the VND because the CVA/DVA also changes in the same direction. If yields fall, the VND goes up; the CVA/DVA also goes up because the expected loss due to default is increased even if the default probability and recovery rate are unchanged. If yields go up, the VND and CVA/DVA both decrease. This suggests that risk-free government bond prices are more volatile than comparable corporate bond prices.

- A change in the assumed volatility of the benchmark interest rate has a small impact on the fair value of corporate bonds. The VND doesn't change (because the benchmark discount factors do not change) but the CVA/DVA does via the expected exposure to loss from issuer default.
- The curve (i.e., effective) duration of a fixed-rate bond, which is calculated by shifting the benchmark yield curve up and down and calculating the new fair values, is greater than the modified yield duration when the benchmark yield curve is upward-sloping. This is also true for the curve and yield convexity statistics.
- The binomial forward rate tree and credit risk models can be used to value floating-rate notes, with and without embedded options (i.e., caps and floors on the periodic interest payments) as well as standalone interest rate options. These have unilateral credit risk and the fair value is the VND minus the CVA/DVA. A capped floater can be interpreted as a combination of a straight floater and an interest rate cap.
- The effective duration of a floating-rate note is close to zero and can be slightly negative if the security is priced at a discount below par value. That indicates positive correlation between benchmark yields and the price of the floater, which is a rare phenomenon with debt securities.
- The binomial tree and credit risk models can be used to value a callable bond under the assumption of constant credit risk over time, thereby underestimating the value of the embedded option. Given the fair value of the callable bond, the option-adjusted yield and spread (the OAS) can be calculated in addition to the bond's effective duration and convexity. The effective duration of a callable bond is always lower than an otherwise comparable non-callable bond.
- The impact of a change in interest rate volatility on callable bonds and capped floating-rate notes is more pronounced than on traditional fixed-rate debt because of the embedded options.
- Credit risk on an uncollateralized interest rate swap is bilateral in that both counterparties need to be concerned with possible default by the other. The fair value of a swap is the VND *minus*

the CVA (the credit risk of the counterparty) *plus* the DVA (the credit risk of the entity itself).

- Even if the VND for a swap is zero and the credit risk parameters (i.e., probability of default and the recovery rate) for the two counterparties are identical, CVA and DVA are not necessarily equal because their respective expected exposures to loss are different if the underlying yield curve is not flat. Therefore the shape of the yield curve is an element in swap pricing, meaning the determination of the fixed rate such that the initial fair value of the swap is zero.

- The objective of collateralization is to drive the CVA and DVA to approach zero by having the recovery rate approach 100% (and the loss severity approach 0%).

- An interest rate swap can be interpreted as a long/short combination of a fixed-rate bond and a floating-rate bond. A pay-fixed swap is comparable to being long a floating-rate bond having the same reference rate as the swap and being short a fixed-rate bond having a coupon rate matching the swap fixed rate, and vice versa for a received-fixed swap. The market value of the swap can be inferred by the difference in the values of the two implicit bonds. However, this combination-of-bonds produces an accurate VND for the swap but is only an estimate of the fair value because the CVA and DVA of the fixed-rate and floating-rate bonds are different than the CVA and DVA of the swap. The source of the difference is the treatment of the redemption of principal for the bonds in calculating the expected exposure to default loss.

- An interest rate swap also can be interpreted as a long/short combination of an interest rate cap and a floor, each having the same strike rate as the fixed rate on the swap. A pay-fixed swap generates the same cash flows (assuming no default) as owning an interest rate cap and writing the floor. A receive-fixed swap is comparable to a long position in the floor and a short position in the cap. The cap-floor combination also produces an accurate VND for the swap but a slightly different fair value. The expected exposures (and CVAs and DVAs) on caps and floors are much more similar to those on swaps than are those for fixed- and floating-rate bonds because the principal on these derivatives is notional.

- The effective duration for an interest rate swap can be calculated by shifting the underlying benchmark bond par curve up and down by the same amount, calibrating new binomial forward rate trees, and calculating the new fair values. Because the market value of a swap is relatively small in relation to the notional principal (and typically zero at initiation), the effective duration statistic can be quite large. An alternative is to use the basis-point-value (BPV), which is the effective duration times the market value, times one basis point.

- The BPV for a swap can be calculated directly using the effective duration. It also can be inferred from the combination of implicit fixed-rate and floating-rate bonds and from the cap-floor combination. The cap-floor combination produces a closer result than the combination of bonds because the credit risk on a swap is closer to that of caps and floors.

- A funding valuation adjustment (FVA) can arise in an interest rate swap portfolio due to collateralization. Cash that is posted to counterparties or a central clearing-house earns a lower interest rate (in practice the OIS rate, in the book the 1-year benchmark rate) than the bank's cost of funds. Banks obtain funds in the money market paying rates that reflect their probabilities of default and recovery rates. Posting collateral represents a funding cost. On the other hand, when banks receive cash collateral, they pay only the lower interest rate. That generates a funding benefit.

- There are multiple ways to calculate the FVA. One method is to solve for the "haircut" using the expected receipts and postings of cash collateral and the bank's credit risk parameters. Another method is to project future money market rates using the benchmark forward rates in the binomial tree. The FVA is based on the difference between the money market and benchmark rates (i.e., the credit spread) and the expected receipts and postings of cash collateral.

- The valuation model can be used to illustrate the novel risk statistics on structured notes. An inverse floater that pays a fixed rate minus the benchmark reference rate has higher effective duration and convexity than a comparable fixed-rate bond. A bear floater that pays a multiple to the reference rate minus a fixed rate has negative effective duration and convexity.

References

Adams, James and Donald J. Smith, "Mind the Gap: Using Derivatives Overlays to Hedge Pension Duration, *Financial Analysts Journal*, Vol. 65, No. 4, July/August 2009, pp. 60–67.

Adams, James and Donald J. Smith, "Synthetic Floating-Rate Debt: An Example of an Asset-Driven Liability Structure," *Journal of Applied Corporate Finance*, Vol. 25, No. 4, Fall 2013.

Brown, Keith C. and Donald J. Smith, *Interest Rate and Currency Swaps: A Tutorial*, Research Foundation of the Institute for Chartered Financial Analysts, 1995; available at the CFA Institute website.

Buetow, Jr., Gerald W. and James Sochacki, *Term-Structure Models Using Binomial Trees*, The Research Foundation of AIMR (now The CFA Institute), Charlottesville, VA, 2001.

Cox, John C., Stephen A. Ross, and Mark Rubenstein, "Option Pricing: A Simplified Approach," *Journal of Financial Economics*, Vol. 7, September 1979, pp. 229–263.

Duffie, Darrell and Kenneth J. Singleton, *Credit Risk: Pricing, Measurement, and Management*, Princeton University Press, Princeton, NJ, 2003.

Fabozzi, Frank J., *Fixed Income Analysis*, 2nd Edition, John Wiley & Sons, Inc., Hoboken, NJ, 2007.

Fabozzi, Frank J., *Bond Markets, Analysis and Strategies*, 8th Edition, Pearson Education, Upper Saddle River, NJ, 2013.

Finnerty, John D., "Adjusting the Binomial Model for Default Risk," *Journal of Portfolio Management*, Vol. 25, No. 2, Winter 1999, pp. 93–103.

Finnerty, John D. and Douglas R. Emery, *Debt Management*, Harvard Business School Press, Boston, MA, 2001.

Green, Andrew, *XVA: Credit, Funding and Capital Valuation Adjustments*, Wiley, 2015.

Gregory, Jon, *Counterparty Credit Risk*, John Wiley & Sons, Ltd., West Sussex, UK, 2010.

Gregory, Jon, *The xVA Challenge: Counterparty Credit Risk, Funding, Collateral, and Capital*, 3rd edition, Wiley, 2015.

Hull, John C., *Options, Futures, and Other Derivatives*, 6th Edition, Pearson Education, Upper Saddle River, NJ, 2006.

Hull, John C. and Alan White, "The FVA Debate", *Risk*, 25th Anniversary Edition, 2012, pp. 83–85.

Hull, John C. and Alan White, "LIBOR vs. OIS: The Derivatives Discounting Dilemma," *Journal of Investment Management*, Vol. 11, No. 3 (2013), pp. 14–27.

Hull, John C. and Alan White, "Valuing Derivatives: Funding Value Adjustments and Fair Value," *Financial Analysts Journal*, Vol. 70, No. 3, May-June 2014, pp. 46–56.

Kalotay, Andrew J., George O. Williams and Frank J. Fabozzi, "A Model for Valuing Bonds and Embedded Options," *Financial Analysts Journal*, Vol. 49, No. 3, May-June 1993, pp. 35–46.

Lu, Dongsheng, *The XVA of Financial Derivatives: CVA, DVA and FVA Explained*, Palgrave Macmillan, 2015.

KPMG, "FVA — Putting Funding into the Equation", 2013. Available at: http://www.kpmg.com/UK/en/IssuesAndInsights/ ArticlesPublications/Pages/funding-valuation-adjustments.aspx.

Miller, Tom, *Introduction to Option-Adjusted Spread Analysis*, 3rd Edition, Bloomberg Press, New York, NY, 2007.

Ruiz, Ignacio, *XVA Desks — A New Era for Risk Management: Understanding, Building and Managing Counterparty*, Funding and Capital Risk, Palgrave Macmillan, 2015.

Ruiz, Ignacio, "The New Economics of OTC Derivatives," 2016, manuscript available at iruizconsulting.com

Smith, Donald J., "The Pricing of Bull and Bear Floating Rate Notes: An Application of Financial Engineering," *Financial Management*, Vol. 17, No. 4, Winter 1988, pp. 72–81.

Smith, Donald J., "The Arithmetic of Financial Engineering," *Journal of Applied Corporate Finance*, Vol. 1, No. 4, Winter 1989, pp. 49–58.

Smith, Donald J., "Negative Duration: The Odd Case of GMAC's Floating-Rate Note," *Journal of Applied Finance*, Vol. 16, No. 2, Fall/Winter 2006, pp. 37–44.

Smith, Donald J., "Valuing Interest Rate Swaps Using Overnight Indexed Swap (OIS) Discounting," *The Journal of Derivatives*, Vol. 20, No. 4, Summer 2013, pp. 49–59.

Smith, Donald J. *Bond Math: The Theory Behind the Formulas*, 2nd Edition, Wiley Finance, Hoboken, NJ, 2014.

Smith, Donald J., "Understanding CVA, DVA, and FVA: Examples of Interest Rate Swap Valuation," revised September 2015. Available at SSRN: http://ssrn.com/abstract=2510970.

Smith, Donald J. *Valuation in a World of CVA and DVA: A Tutorial on Debt Securities and Interest Rate Derivatives*, self-published manuscript by CreateSpace (an Amazon subsidiary), 2015.

Tuckman, Bruce and Angel Serrat, *Fixed Income Securities: Tools for Today's Markets*, 3rd Edition, Wiley Finance, Hoboken, NJ, 2012.

Appendix

The Forward Rate Binomial Tree Model

This book uses a *one-factor binomial forward rate tree* model for the term structure of interest rates to illustrate the impact of CVA, DVA, and FVA on the valuation of debt securities and derivatives. The one factor is the short-term interest rate. That means that all interest rate volatility is realized through changes in the short-term rate. To keep the model simple, this is assumed to be the 1-year rate and the underlying benchmark bonds are assumed to make annual coupon payments. In particular, the forward rate trees are based on the Kalotay-Williams-Fabozzi (KWF) model.[1] Buetow and Sochacki (2001) provide a detailed review of this and other one-factor term structure models, including the Ho-Lee, Hull-While, Black-Karasinski, and Black-Derman-Toy models. The KWF model is chosen for this introduction to valuing risky bonds and derivatives because it is familiar to many finance professionals in that it has been used in the CFA® (Chartered Financial Analyst) examination readings since 2000.

Exhibit A-1 displays the primary binomial tree that is used. The initial 1-year rate on Date 0 is 1.0000%. At the end of the first year on Date 1, the 1-year rate for the second year will be either 3.6326% or 2.4350%. An important feature to this model is that the odds of the rate going up or down are assumed to be 50-50 for all nodes in the tree. Below each forward rate in parenthesis is the probability of attaining that particular node in the tree. On Date 2 at the end of the second year, the possible 1-year forward rates are 5.1111%, 3.4261%,

Exhibit A-1: Binomial Forward Rate Tree for 20% Volatility

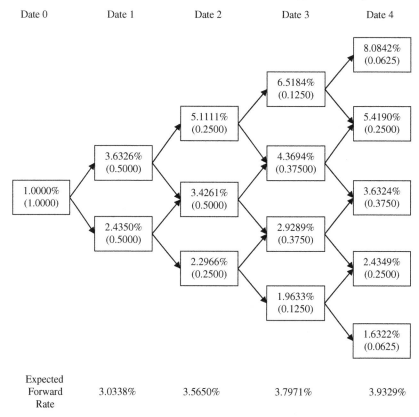

and 2.2966% with probabilities of 0.25, 0.50, and 0.25, respectively. This is a *recombinant* tree in that the 3.4261% outcome could have been obtained from the 1-year rate initially having gone up or down. [Note that "up" and "down" refer to the relative movement at each node without regard to the actual change in the interest rate.]

This forward rate tree is derived from an underlying sequence of arbitrarily chosen annual coupon payment, risk-free benchmark government bonds. "Risk-free" here is with respect to default risk but not inflation risk—presumably the government issuer can and will print money to assure that there is no default to the bondholder. The coupon rates and prices for these bonds are given in Exhibit A-2.

Exhibit A-2: Underlying Benchmark Coupon Rates, Prices, and Yields to Maturity

Date	Coupon Rate	Price	Yield to Maturity
1	1.00%	100	1.00%
2	2.00%	100	2.00%
3	2.50%	100	2.50%
4	2.80%	100	2.80%
5	3.00%	100	3.00%

This is the *par curve* for the benchmark bonds out to five years in that each bond is priced at par value so that the coupon rate equals the yield to maturity. Also, there is no accrued interest because the time to maturity is an integer.

The next step is to bootstrap the discount factors corresponding to each date. A *discount factor* is the present value of one unit of currency received at a future date. The Date-1 discount factor, denoted DF_1, is simply $1/1.010000 = 0.990099$ because the 1-year rate is 1.0000%. The bootstrapping technique requires an initial zero-coupon bond to launch the procedure. Typically, this comes from the money market, for instance, the yield on a short-term Treasury bill. Here the 1-year annual payment bond implicitly provides the starting point.

The Date-2 discount factor is the solution for DF_2 in this equation:

$$100 = (2 * 0.990099) + (102 * DF_2), \quad DF_2 = 0.960978$$

Note that the future cash flows on the 2-year, 2% bond are 2 and 102 and the price is 100. Similarly, the Date-3 discount factor is the solution for DF_3, whereby the results from the previous steps are used as inputs — that is the hallmark of bootstrapping. The cash flows on the 3-year, 2.5% bond are 2.5, 2.5, and 102.5 and the price is again 100.

$$100 = (2.5 * 0.990099) + (2.5 * 0.960978)$$
$$+ (102.5 * DF_3), \quad DF_3 = 0.928023$$

To generalize, the discount factor for the nth date (DF_n) is:

$$DF_n = \frac{1 - CR_n * \sum_{j=1}^{n-1} DF_j}{1 + CR_n} \qquad (A1)$$

CR_n is the coupon rate for the n-year bond on the par curve.

The implied spot (or zero-coupon) rates that correspond to the discount factors are easily calculated. The "$0 \times n$" spot rate, meaning a rate that starts on Date 0 and ends on Date n and is denoted $Spot_{0,n}$, is calculated using this formula:

$$Spot_{0,n} = \left(\frac{1}{DF_n}\right)^{1/n} - 1 \qquad (A2)$$

For example, the 3-year ("0×3") implied spot rate is 2.5212%.

$$Spot_{0,3} = \left(\frac{1}{0.928023}\right)^{1/3} - 1 = 0.025212$$

The implied spot rates are used to validate the accuracy of the valuations produced using the binomial tree model and to calculate spreads over the benchmark rates.

The implied forward, or projected, rates are also calculated from the series of discount factors. For the forward rate between Date $n-1$ and Date n, denoted $Forward_{n-1,n}$, this formula is used:

$$Forward_{n-1,n} = \frac{DF_{n-1}}{DF_n} - 1 \qquad (A3)$$

As an example, the 1-year rate, two years forward, is 3.5512%. It is the 1-year rate between Dates 2 and 3. It can be called the "2×3" forward rate; in practice, this rate sometimes is designated the "2y1y" rate.

$$Forward_{2,3} = \frac{0.960978}{0.928023} - 1 = 0.035512$$

These forward rates are the baseline around which the binomial tree is built.[2] The series of discount rates, spot rates, and forward rates are shown in Exhibit A-3.

Exhibit A-3: Discount Factors, Spot Rates, and Forward Rates

Time Frame	Discount Factor	Spot Rate
0×1	0.990099	1.0000%
0×2	0.960978	2.0101%
0×3	0.928023	2.5212%
0×4	0.894344	2.8310%
0×5	0.860968	3.0392%

Time Frame	Forward Rate
0×1	1.0000%
1×2	3.0303%
2×3	3.5512%
3×4	3.7658%
4×5	3.8766%

Before describing the process by which the binomial tree is derived, notice that for each date the *implied* forward rates in Exhibit A-3 are lower than the *expected* forward rates in Exhibit A-1. The 1-year implied forward rate for the timespan between Date 4 and Date 5 is 3.8766%, whereas the expected rate given the five possible outcomes and their probabilities is 3.9329%.

$$(8.0842\% * 0.0625) + (5.4190\% * 0.2500) + (3.6324\% * 0.3750)$$
$$+ (2.4349\% * 0.2500) + (1.6322\% * 0.0625) = 3.9329\%$$

This difference arises because the KWF model assumes a *log-normal* distribution for the forward rate. This assumption alleviates the problem of negative nominal rates present in some term structure models (e.g., Ho-Lee and Hull-White) that use a normal distribution for the rates. Log-normality means that the *percentage change* in rates is normally distributed. Therefore, the rates in the tree for each date are not distributed symmetrically around the forward rate. When volatilty is increased, the rates at the top of the tree go up more than the rates at the bottom go down.

The log-normality assumption is particularly important when interest rates are at historic lows. While negative *real rates* can and do occur, it is not common (but not impossible as we have seen recently in some Asian and Eurozone markets) for *nominal rates* to go below zero, especially on uncollateralized interbank borrowing and lending rates such as LIBOR. In any case, it is possible to adjust the model to allow rates to become negative but that goes beyond this introduction to valuation.

The binomial forward rate tree is designed to branch out around the implied forward rate for each date. This is illustrated in Exhibit A-4; the dotted line is the forward curve. For example, the Date-1 rates of 3.6326% and 2.4350% are above and below the "1 × 2" implied forward rate of 3.0303%. How much above and below depends critically on the assumed annual volatility. This tree assumes a constant annual standard deviation of 20% for each year.

The KWF model is among the class known as *arbitrage-free* term structure models because it is calibrated to assure that the valuation obtained for each benchmark bond matches the market price, which is assumed to be par value.[3] Using the log-normal distribution for

Exhibit A-4: The Binomial Tree Branches Out around the Forward Curve

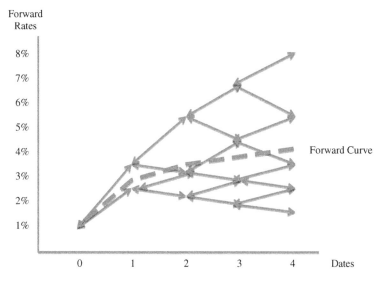

the forward rate, the initial trials for Date-1 rates moving up and down are given by:

$$3.0303\% * \exp\left(-\frac{0.04}{2} + 0.20\right) = 3.0303\% * 1.197217 = 3.6279\%$$

$$3.0303\% * \exp\left(-\frac{0.04}{2} - 0.20\right) = 3.0303\% * 0.802519 = 2.4319\%$$

The general expression for this pattern, whereby σ is the assumed annual standard deviation for the forward rate and T is the relevant time period, is:

$$\text{Forward Rate} * \exp\left(-\frac{\sigma^2 * T}{2} \pm \sigma * \sqrt{T}\right) \qquad \text{(A4)}$$

In this simplified example, σ is 0.20 and T is 1.

These initial rates of 3.6279% and 2.4319% are then tested and calibrated using the *backward induction* method of valuation to eliminate any arbitrage opportunity. This is illustrated in the upper panel to Exhibit A-5. Notice that the scheduled cash flows on the 2-year benchmark bond (per 100 of par value) are placed directly across from the node on the binomial tree. The first coupon payment of 2 on Date 1 is across from the Date-0 rate of 1.0000%. The final coupon payment and principal redemption for a total of 102 are across from the two possible Date-1 forward rates. If the 1-year rate goes up to 3.6279% from 1.0000%, the value of the bond on Date 1 is 98.4291 (= 102/1.036279). If the rate goes "down" to 2.4319%, the bond value is 99.5784 (= 102/1.024319).

The next step is critical to understanding how backward induction works. The key assumption is that the value of the bond on Date 0 is the present value of the expected value on Date 1, assuming at the probability of the rate going up is 0.50 and probability of rate going down is also 0.50. Those 50-50 odds make the calculations easy — that is why the discrete version of the KWF binomial model is so useful for pedagogy. The expected value of the bond on Date 1 is [2 + (0.50 * 98.4291 + 0.50 * 99.5784)], the scheduled coupon payment plus the probability-weighted average of the two possible prices. Discounting that amount back to Date 0 using the 1-year

Exhibit A-5: Calibrating the Forward Rates on the Binomial Tree for Date 1

Upper Panel: The Initial Test

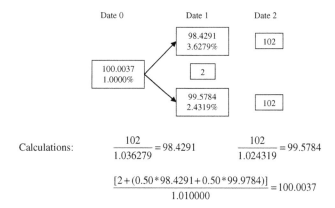

Lower Panel: The Final Calibration

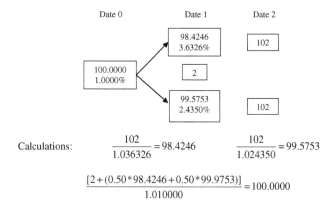

rate of 1.0000% gives 100.0037

$$\frac{[2 + (0.50 * 98.4291 + 0.50 * 99.5784)]}{1.010000} = 100.0037$$

The problem is that this price is too high because the 2-year bond needs to be priced at par value (specifically, 100.0000) to meet the no-arbitrage condition.

These two trial forward rates for Date 1 need to be increased a bit to get the present value down to 100.0000. But, importantly, they need to be raised proportionately to preserve constant volatility. Given log-normality and the assumed annual standard deviation of 20%, the ratio of the up and down rates emanating from each node in the tree is 1.491825. The general relationship is:

$$\frac{\exp\left(-\frac{\sigma^2 * T}{2} + \sigma * \sqrt{T}\right)}{\exp\left(-\frac{\sigma^2 * T}{2} - \sigma * \sqrt{T}\right)} = \frac{\exp\left(-\frac{\sigma^2 * T}{2}\right) * \exp(\sigma * \sqrt{T})}{\exp\left(-\frac{\sigma^2 * T}{2}\right) * \exp(-\sigma * \sqrt{T})}$$

$$= \exp(2 * \sigma * \sqrt{T}) \qquad (A5)$$

For $\sigma = 0.20$ and $T = 1$, $\exp(0.40) = 1.491825$. The calibration process entails raising the rates by a small amount until the price rounds off to 100.0000 while keeping the proportionality factor. This final result is shown in the lower panel of Exhibit A-5 — the two possible rates for the 1-year bond on Date 1 turn out to be 3.6326% and 2.4350%. [Note that all calculations are done on a spreadsheet to preserve precision and the rounded values are shown for consistency in presentation.]

Now the model builder moves out to Date 2. This is displayed in Exhibit A-6. The three initial forward rates in upper panel are 5.2978%, 3.5512%, and 2.3804%. The middle rate is the implied forward rate between Dates 2 and 3 given in Exhibit A-3. The first and third rates are set to preserve constant 20% volatility: 3.5512% * 1.491825 = 5.2978% and 3.5512%/1.491825 = 2.3804%. Working through the tree using backward induction produces a price on the 3-year, 2.50% annual coupon payment bond of 99.8814, which is below the no-arbitrage target price of 100.0000. Lowering the initial rates proportionately by trial and error (or using Solver in Excel) eventually leads to a price that rounds to 100.0000. Those rates, shown in the lower panel of Exhibit A-6, are 5.1111%, 3.4261%, and 2.2966%.[a]

---

[a]Because the rates are rounded to four digits, the ratio between adjoining rates is not always exactly equal to 1.491825. For instance, 3.4261%/2.2966% = 1.491814.

Exhibit A-6: Calibrating the Forward Rates on the Binomial Tree for Date 2

Upper Panel: The Initial Test

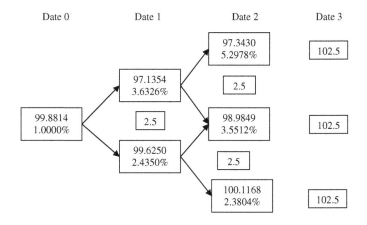

Lower Panel: The Final Calibration

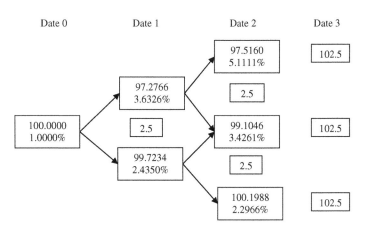

The next step is to get trial rates for Date 3, taking the calibrated Date-1 and Date-2 rates (rounded to four decimals) as inputs. The general pattern is to use the implied forward rate for the middle rate when the number of nodes for the date is odd, for instance, three nodes for Date 2 and five nodes for Date 4. Then the other trial rates are set using the proportionality factor to preserve constant volatility.

When the number of nodes is even, for instance, two nodes for Date 1 and four nodes for Date 3, the implied forward rate is adjusted up or down, as demonstrated above for the Date-1 calibration.

Exhibit A-7 shows the initial test and final calibration trees for Date 3. The initial rates are 6.7258%, 4.5084%, 3.0221% and 2.0258%. These spread out around the "3 × 4" forward rate of 3.7658%, which is shown in Exhibit A-3. The middle two rates are calculated as for Date 1:

$$3.7658\% * \exp\left(-\frac{0.04}{2} + 0.20\right) = 3.7658\% * 1.197217 = 4.5084\%$$

$$3.7658\% * \exp\left(-\frac{0.04}{2} - 0.20\right) = 3.7658\% * 0.802519 = 3.0221\%$$

The outer two rates follow from these: $4.5084\% * 1.491825 = 6.7258\%$ and $3.0221\%/1.491825 = 2.0258\%$, using the proportionality factor for 20% volatility. The trial rates produce a value of 99.8944 for the 2.80%, 4-year benchmark bond. After lowering them a bit — and keeping them proportional — the final rates of 6.5184%, 4.3694%, 2.9289%, and 1.9633% result in a value of 100.0000 for the bond.

The initial test rates for Date 4 start with the "4 × 5" forward rate of 3.8766%. These are shown in Exhibit A-8. The rates above and below preserve proportionality: $3.8766\% * 1.491825 = 5.7831\%$, $5.7831\% * 1.491825 = 8.6274\%$, $3.8766\%/1.491825 = 2.5985\%$, and $2.5985\%/1.491825 = 1.7419\%$. [Note: the spreadsheet behind these numbers uses the full precision proportionality factor, $\exp(0.40)$]. The value for the 3%, 5-year benchmark bond turns out to be 99.7795. Trial-and-error search leads to Date-4 rates of 8.0842%, 5.4190%, 3.6324%, 2.4349%, and 1.6322%. These value the benchmark bond at par value.

This "artisanal" approach to model-building, in particular, bootstrapping the forward curve and calibrating the rates in the tree year by year, is intended to reinforce the idea of no arbitrage. In practice a computer model can be built to get the tree instananeously and without rounding the rates to four digits. In any case, once the tree is developed, it can be used in applications other than valuation. For example, the sensitivity of the total return facing a buy-and-hold

Exhibit A-7: Calibrating the Forward Rates on the Binomial Tree for Date 3

Upper Panel: The Initial Test

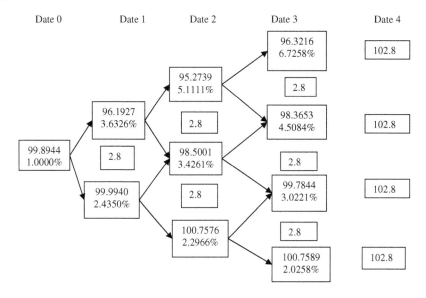

Lower Panel: The Final Calibration

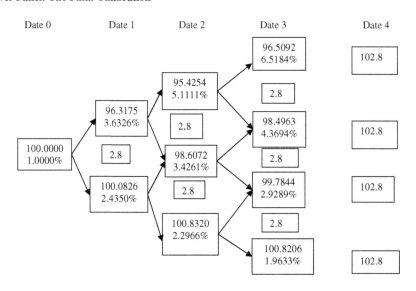

Exhibit A-8: Calibrating the Forward Rates on the Binomial Tree for Date 4

Upper Panel: The Initial Test

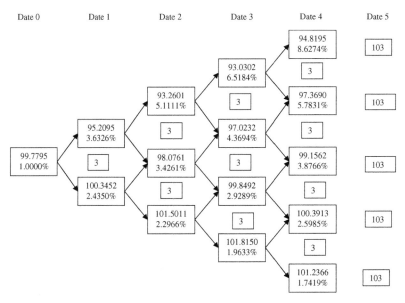

Lower Panel: The Final Calibration

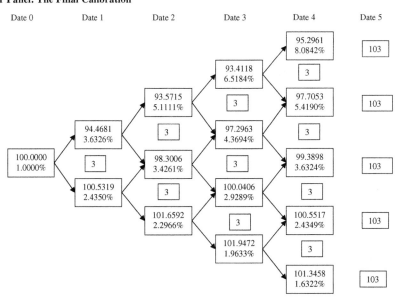

investor in the 5-year benchmark bond to coupon reinvestment risk can be analyzed along each possible path. For example, suppose that the 1-year rate tracks the topmost path in the tree so that coupon payments can be reinvested each year at 3.6326%, 5.1111%, 6.5184%, and 8.0842%, respectively.

The 5-year total return is 117.0891 per 100 of par value.

$$((((((3*1.036326)+3)*1.05111)+3)*1.065184)+3)$$
$$*1.080842 + 103 = 117.0891$$

The 5-year holding-period rate of return is 3.2056% along this particular path, found as the solution for "rate" in this expression:

$$100 = \frac{117.0891}{(1+\text{rate})^5}, \quad \text{rate} = 0.032056$$

This is 20.56 basis points higher than the 3.00% yield to maturity on the 5-year benchmark bond. However, the probability of realizing this path is only 0.0625, as shown in Exhibit A-1. The range of possible total returns that are consistent with the model and the assumption of 20% volatility can calculated in the same manner.

In summary, the KWF model used in this tutorial is a one-factor model of the term structure of interest rates. Movement in the short-term rate, here the 1-year rate, is only factor driving volatility in interest rates. The model assumes constant volatility in that the up and down rates branching out from each node maintain the same ratio. The model also assumes that the forward rates follow a lognormal distribution. That assumption means that the expected forward rates are above the implied forward rates. Finally, the KWF model assumes no arbitrage in that it is calibrated to price correctly the underlying benchmark bonds.

Endnotes to the Appendix

1. The original source for the KWF model is a 1993 article by Kalotay, Williams, and Fabozzi in the *Financial Analysts Journal*. It is described and used in various Fabozzi textbooks, including *Fixed Income Analysis* and *Fixed Income Markets, Analysis, and Strategies*, as well as in a 2001 practitioner-oriented textbook by Finnerty and Emery. Another useful

resource is a 2007 book by Miller, which describes the version of the model that is used by Bloomberg.

2. Equations (A1), (A2), and (A3) are simplified because of the annual coupon payment assumption. These are the general formulas whereby A_j and A_n are the day-count fractions for the jth and n^{th} period:

$$DF_n = \frac{1 - CR_n * \sum_{j=1}^{n-1} DF_j * A_j}{1 + CR_n * A_n}$$

$$Spot_n = \left[\left(\frac{1}{DF_n}\right)^{1/n} - 1\right] * \frac{1}{A_n}$$

$$Forward_{n-1,n} = \left[\frac{DF_{n-1}}{DF_n} - 1\right] * \frac{1}{A_n}$$

For example, if the underlying bonds make semiannual payments and the day-count convention is actual/actual, A_j might be 181/365 and A_n 184/365. In practice, daily discount factors are needed to value the multitude of debt securities and derivatives that are on a financial institution's balance sheet, thereby requiring interpolation between rates and prices on observed bonds.

3. Tuckman and Serrat (2012) provide a thorough discussion of term structure models, the differences between equilibrium and arbitrage-free models, and the multi-factor models that are used in practice, including the LIBOR Market Model.